Natural Language Processing Recipes

Unlocking Text Data with Machine Learning and Deep Learning Using Python

Second Edition

Akshay Kulkarni
Adarsha Shivananda

Apress®

Natural Language Processing Recipes: Unlocking Text Data with Machine Learning and Deep Learning Using Python

Akshay Kulkarni
Bangalore, Karnataka, India

Adarsha Shivananda
Bangalore, Karnataka, India

ISBN-13 (pbk): 978-1-4842-7350-0
https://doi.org/10.1007/978-1-4842-7351-7

ISBN-13 (electronic): 978-1-4842-7351-7

Managing Director, Apress Media LLC: Welmoed Spahr
Acquisitions Editor: Celestin Suresh John
Development Editor: Laura Berendson
Coordinating Editor: Shrikant Vishwakarma

Cover designed by eStudioCalamar

Cover image designed by Pexels

Distributed to the book trade worldwide by Springer Science+Business Media LLC, 1 New York Plaza, Suite 4600, New York, NY 10004. Phone 1-800-SPRINGER, fax (201) 348-4505, email orders-ny@springer-sbm. com, or visit www.springeronline.com. Apress Media, LLC is a California LLC and the sole member (owner) is Springer Science + Business Media Finance Inc (SSBM Finance Inc). SSBM Finance Inc is a **Delaware** corporation.

For information on translations, please e-mail booktranslations@springernature.com; for reprint, paperback, or audio rights, please e-mail bookpermissions@springernature.com, or visit http://www.apress.com/rights-permissions.

Apress titles may be purchased in bulk for academic, corporate, or promotional use. eBook versions and licenses are also available for most titles. For more information, reference our Print and eBook Bulk Sales web page at http://www.apress.com/bulk-sales.

Any source code or other supplementary material referenced by the author in this book is available to readers on GitHub via the book's product page, located at www.apress.com/978-1-4842-7350-0. For more detailed information, please visit http://www.apress.com/source-code.

Printed on acid-free paper

To our families

Table of Contents

About the Authors

Akshay Kulkarni is a renowned AI and machine learning evangelist and thought leader. He has consulted several Fortune 500 and global enterprises on driving AI and data science–led strategic transformation. Akshay has rich experience in building and scaling AI and machine learning businesses and creating significant impact. He is currently a data science and AI manager at Publicis Sapient, where he is part of strategy and transformation interventions through AI. He manages high-priority growth initiatives around data science and works on various artificial intelligence engagements by applying state-of-the-art techniques to this space.

Akshay is also a Google Developers Expert in machine learning, a published author of books on NLP and deep learning, and a regular speaker at major AI and data science conferences.

In 2019, Akshay was named one of the top "40 under 40 data scientists" in India.

In his spare time, he enjoys reading, writing, coding, and mentoring aspiring data scientists. He lives in Bangalore, India, with his family.

Adarsha Shivananda is a lead data scientist at Indegene Inc.'s product and technology team, where he leads a group of analysts who enable predictive analytics and AI features to healthcare software products. These are mainly multichannel activities for pharma products and solving the real-time problems encountered by pharma sales reps. Adarsha aims to build a pool of exceptional data scientists within the organization to solve greater health care problems through brilliant training programs. He always wants to stay ahead of the curve.

His core expertise involves machine learning, deep learning, recommendation systems, and statistics. Adarsha has worked on various data science projects across multiple domains using different technologies and methodologies. Previously, he worked for Tredence Analytics and IQVIA.

He lives in Bangalore, India, and loves to read, ride, and teach data science.

About the Technical Reviewer

 **Aakash Kag** is a data scientist at AlixPartners and is a co-founder of the Emeelan application. He has six years of experience in big data analytics and has a postgraduate degree in computer science with a specialization in big data analytics. Aakash is passionate about developing social platforms, machine learning, and meetups, where he often talks.

Acknowledgments

We are grateful to our families for their motivation and constant support.

We want to express our gratitude to out mentors and friends for their input, inspiration, and support. A special thanks to Anoosh R. Kulkarni, a data scientist at Quantziq, for his support in writing this book and his technical input. A big thanks to the Apress team for their constant support and help.

Finally, we would like to thank you, the reader, for showing an interest in this book and making your natural language processing journey more exciting.

Note that the views and opinions expressed in this book are those of the authors.

Introduction

According to industry estimates, more than 80% of the data being generated is in an unstructured format in the form of text, images, audio, or video. Data is being generated as we speak, write, tweet, use social media platforms, send messages on messaging platforms, use ecommerce to shop, and do various other activities. The majority of this data exists in textual form.

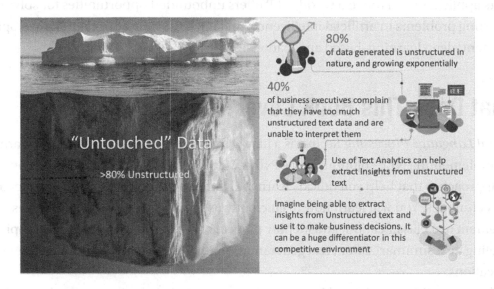

So, what is unstructured data? Unstructured data is information that doesn't reside in a traditional relational database. Examples include documents, blogs, social media feeds, pictures, and videos.

Most of the insights are locked within different types of unstructured data. Unlocking unstructured data plays a vital role in every organization wanting to make improved and better decisions. This book unlocks the potential of textual data.

Textual data is the most common and comprises more than 50% of unstructured data. Examples include tweets/posts on social media, chat conversations, news, blogs, articles, product or services reviews, and patient records in the healthcare sector. Recent examples include voice-driven bots like Siri and Alexa.

To retrieve significant and actionable insights from textual data and unlock its potential, we use natural language processing coupled with machine learning and deep learning.

But what is natural language processing? Machines and algorithms do not understand text or characters, so it is very important to convert textual data into a machine-understandable format (like numbers or binary) to analyze it. *Natural language processing* (NLP) allows machines to understand and interpret the human language.

If you want to use the power of unstructured text, this book is the right starting point. This book unearths the concepts and implementation of natural language processing and its applications in the real world. NLP offers unbounded opportunities for solving interesting problems in artificial intelligence, making it the latest frontier for developing intelligent, deep learning–based applications.

What Does This Book Cover?

Natural Language Processing Recipes is a handy problem/solution reference for learning and implementing NLP solutions using Python. The book is packed with lots of code and approaches that help you quickly learn and implement both basic and advanced NLP techniques. You will learn how to efficiently use a wide range of NLP packages, implement text classification, and identify parts of speech. You also learn about topic modeling, text summarization, text generation, sentiment analysis, and many other NLP applications.

This new edition of *Natural Language Processing Recipes* focuses on implementing end-to-end projects using Python and leveraging cutting-edge algorithms and transfer learning.

The book begins by discussing text data collections, web scraping, and different types of data sources. You learn how to clean and preprocess text data and analyze it using advanced algorithms. Throughout the book, you explore the semantic as well as syntactic analysis of text. It covers complex NLP solutions that involve text normalization, various advanced preprocessing methods, part-of-speech (POS) tagging, parsing, text summarization, sentiment analysis, topic modeling, named-entity recognition (NER), word2vec, seq2seq, and more.

The book covers both fundamental and state-of-the-art techniques used in machine learning applications and deep learning natural language processing. This edition includes various advanced techniques to convert text to features, like GloVe, ELMo, and BERT. It also explains how transformers work, using Sentence-BERT and GPT as examples.

The book closes by discussing some of the advanced industrial applications of NLP with a solution approach and implementation, also leveraging the power of deep learning techniques for natural language processing and natural language generation problems, employing advanced RNNs, like long short-term memory, to solve complex text generation tasks. It also explores embeddings—high-quality representations of words in a language.

In this second edition, few advanced state-of-art embeddings and industrial applications are explained along with end-to-end implementation using deep learning.

Each chapter includes several code examples and illustrations.

By the end of the book, you will have a clear understanding of implementing natural language processing. You will have worked on multiple examples that implement NLP techniques in the real world. Readers will be comfortable with various NLP techniques coupled with machine learning and deep learning and its industrial applications, making the NLP journey much more interesting and improving your Python coding skills.

Who This Book Is For

This book explains various concepts and implementations to get more clarity when applying NLP algorithms to chosen data. You learn about all the ingredients you need to become successful in the NLP space. Fundamental Python skills are assumed, as well as some knowledge of machine learning and basic NLP. If you are an NLP or machine learning enthusiast and an intermediate Python programmer who wants to quickly master natural language processing, this learning path will do you a lot of good.

All you need to know are the basics of machine learning and Python to enjoy the book.

What You Will Learn

- The core concepts of implementing NLP, its various approaches, and using Python libraries such as NLTK, TextBlob, spaCy, and Stanford CoreNLP

- Text preprocessing and feature engineering in NLP along with advanced methods of feature engineering

- Information retrieval, text summarization, sentiment analysis, text classification, and other advanced NLP techniques solved leveraging machine learning and deep learning

- The problems faced by industries and how to implement them using NLP techniques

- Implementing an end-to-end pipeline of NLP life cycle projects, which includes framing the problem, finding the data, collecting, preprocessing the data, and solving it using cutting-edge techniques and tools

What Do You Need for This Book?

To perform all the recipes in this book successfully, you need Python 3.x or higher running on any Windows- or Unix-based operating system with a processor of 2.0 GHz or higher and a minimum of 4 GB RAM. You can download Python from Anaconda and leverage a Jupyter notebook for coding purposes. This book assumes you know Keras basics and how to install the basic machine learning and deep learning libraries.

Please make sure you upgrade or install the latest version of all the libraries.

Python is the most popular and widely used tool for building NLP applications. It has many sophisticated libraries to perform NLP tasks, from basic preprocessing to advanced techniques.

To install any library in a Python Jupyter notebook, use ! before the pip install.

NLTK is a natural language toolkit and is commonly called "the mother of all NLP libraries." It is one of the primary resources when it comes to Python and NLP.

```
!pip install nltk
nltk.download()
```

spaCy is a trending library that comes with the added flavors of a deep learning framework. Although spaCy doesn't cover all NLP functionalities, it does many things well.

```
!pip install spacy
#if above doesn't work, try this in your terminal/ command prompt
conda install spacy
python -m spacy.en.download all
#then load model via
spacy.load('en')
```

TextBlob is one of data scientists' favorite libraries when it comes to implementing NLP tasks. It is based on both NLTK and Pattern. TextBlob isn't the fastest or most complete library, however.

```
!pip install textblob
```

CoreNLP is a Python wrapper for Stanford CoreNLP. The toolkit provides robust, accurate, and optimized techniques for tagging, parsing, and analyzing text in various languages.

```
!pip install CoreNLP
```

There are hundreds of other NLP libraries, but these are the widely used and important ones.

There is an immense number of NLP industrial applications that are leveraged to uncover insights. By the end of the book, you will have implemented many of these use cases, from framing a business problem to building applications and drawing business insights. The following are some examples.

- Sentiment analysis—a customer's emotions toward products offered by the business

- Topic modeling extracts the unique topics from the group of documents.

- Complaint classifications/email classifications/ecommerce product classification, and so on

- Document categorization/management using different clustering techniques.

- Résumé shortlisting and job description matching using similarity methods

- Advanced feature engineering techniques (word2vec and fastText) to capture context

- Information/document retrieval systems, for example, search engines

- Chatbots, Q&A, and voice-to-text applications like Siri, Alexa

- Language detection and translation using neural networks

- Text summarization using graph methods and advanced techniques

- Text generation/predicting the next sequence of words using deep learning algorithms

CHAPTER 1

Extracting the Data

This chapter covers various sources of text data and the ways to extract it. Textual data can act as information or insights for businesses. The following recipes are covered.

- Recipe 1. Text data collection using APIs
- Recipe 2. Reading a PDF file in Python
- Recipe 3. Reading a Word document
- Recipe 4. Reading a JSON object
- Recipe 5. Reading an HTML page and HTML parsing
- Recipe 6. Regular expressions
- Recipe 7. String handling
- Recipe 8. Web scraping

Introduction

Before getting into the details of the book, let's look at generally available data sources. We need to identify potential data sources that can help with solving data science use cases.

Client Data

For any problem statement, one of the sources is the data that is already present. The business decides where it wants to store its data. Data storage depends on the type of business, the amount of data, and the costs associated with the sources. The following are some examples.

1

© Akshay Kulkarni and Adarsha Shivananda 2021
A. Kulkarni and A. Shivananda, *Natural Language Processing Recipes*,
https://doi.org/10.1007/978-1-4842-7351-7_1

- SQL databases

- HDFS

- Cloud storage

- Flat files

Free Sources

A large amount of data is freely available on the Internet. You just need to streamline the problem and start exploring multiple free data sources.

- Free APIs like Twitter

- Wikipedia

- Government data (e.g., http://data.gov)

- Census data (e.g., www.census.gov/data.html)

- Health care claim data (e.g., www.healthdata.gov)

- Data science community websites (e.g., www.kaggle.com)

- Google dataset search (e.g., https://datasetsearch.research.google.com)

Web Scraping

Extracting the content/data from websites, blogs, forums, and retail websites for reviews with permission from the respective sources using web scraping packages in Python.

There are a lot of other sources, such as news data and economic data, that can be leveraged for analysis.

Recipe 1-1. Collecting Data

There are a lot of free APIs through which you can collect data and use it to solve problems. Let's discuss the Twitter API.

Problem

You want to collect text data using Twitter APIs.

Solution

Twitter has a gigantic amount of data with a lot of value in it. Social media marketers make their living from it. There is an enormous number of tweets every day, and every tweet has some story to tell. When all of this data is collected and analyzed, it gives a business tremendous insights about their company, product, service, and so forth.

Let's now look at how to pull data and then explore how to leverage it in the coming chapters.

How It Works

Step 1-1. Log in to the Twitter developer portal

Log in to the Twitter developer portal at `https://developer.twitter.com`.

Create your own app in the Twitter developer portal, and get the following keys. Once you have these credentials, you can start pulling data.

- consumer key: The key associated with the application (Twitter, Facebook, etc.)

- consumer secret: The password used to authenticate with the authentication server (Twitter, Facebook, etc.)

- access token: The key given to the client after successful authentication of keys

- access token secret: The password for the access key

Step 1-2. Execute query in Python

Once all the credentials are in place, use the following code to fetch the data.

```
# Install tweepy
!pip install tweepy

# Import the libraries
```

```
import numpy as np
import tweepy
import json
import pandas as pd
from tweepy import OAuthHandler

# credentials

consumer_key = "adjbiejfaaoeh"
consumer_secret = "had73haf78af"
access_token = "jnsfby5u4yuawhafjeh"
access_token_secret = "jhdfgay768476r"

# calling API

auth = tweepy.OAuthHandler(consumer_key, consumer_secret)
auth.set_access_token(access_token, access_token_secret)
api = tweepy.API(auth)

# Provide the query you want to pull the data. For example, pulling data
for the mobile phone ABC

query ="ABC"

# Fetching tweets

Tweets = api.search(query, count = 10,lang='en',exclude='retweets',
tweet_mode='extended')
```

This query pulls the top ten tweets when product ABC is searched. The API pulls English tweets since the language given is 'en'. It excludes retweets.

Recipe 1-2. Collecting Data from PDFs

Most of your data is stored in PDF files. You need to extract text from these files and store it for further analysis.

Problem

You want to read a PDF file.

Solution

The simplest way to read a PDF file is by using the PyPDF2 library.

How It Works

Follow the steps in this section to extract data from PDF files.

Step 2-1. Install and import all the necessary libraries

Here are the first lines of code.

```
!pip install PyPDF2
import PyPDF2
from PyPDF2 import PdfFileReader
```

Note   You can download any PDF file from the web and place it in the location where you are running this Jupyter notebook or Python script.

Step 2-2. Extract text from a PDF file

Now let's extract the text.

```
#Creating a pdf file object

pdf = open("file.pdf","rb")

#creating pdf reader object

pdf_reader = PyPDF2.PdfFileReader(pdf)

#checking number of pages in a pdf file

print(pdf_reader.numPages)

#creating a page object

page = pdf_reader.getPage(0)

#finally extracting text from the page
```

```
print(page.extractText())

#closing the pdf file

pdf.close()
```

Please note that the function doesn't work for scanned PDFs.

Recipe 1-3. Collecting Data from Word Files

Next, let's look at another small recipe that reads Word files in Python.

Problem

You want to read Word files.

Solution

The simplest way is to use the docx library.

How It Works

Follow the steps in this section to extract data from a Word file.

Step 3-1. Install and import all the necessary libraries

The following is the code to install and import the docx library.

```
#Install docx
!pip install docx

#Import library
from docx import Document
```

Note   You can download any Word file from the web and place it in the location where you are running a Jupyter notebook or Python script.

Step 3-2. Extract text from a Word file

Now let's get the text.

```
#Creating a word file object

doc = open("file.docx","rb")

#creating word reader object

document = docx.Document(doc)

#create an empty string and call this document. #This document variable
stores each paragraph in the Word document.
#We then create a "for" loop that goes through each paragraph in the Word
document and appends the paragraph.

docu=""
for para in document.paragraphs.
        docu += para.text

#to see the output call docu
print(docu)
```

Recipe 1-4. Collecting Data from JSON

JSON is an open standard file format that stands for *JavaScript Object Notation*. It's often used when data is sent to a webpage from a server. This recipe explains how to read a JSON file/object.

Problem

You want to read a JSON file/object.

Solution

The simplest way is to use requests and the JSON library.

How It Works

Follow the steps in this section to extract data from JSON.

Step 4-1. Install and import all the necessary libraries

Here is the code for importing the libraries.

```
import requests
import json
```

Step 4-2. Extract text from a JSON file

Now let's extract the text.

```
#extracting the text from "https://quotes.rest/qod.json"
r = requests.get("https://quotes.rest/qod.json")
res = r.json()
print(json.dumps(res, indent = 4))

#output
{
    "success": {
        "total": 1
    },
    "contents": {
        "quotes": [
            {
                "quote": "Where there is ruin, there is hope for a treasure.",
                "length": "50",
                "author": "Rumi",
                "tags": [
                    "failure",
                    "inspire",
                    "learning-from-failure"
                ],
                "category": "inspire",
                "date": "2018-09-29",
```

```
            "permalink": "https://theysaidso.com/quote/
            dPKsui4sQnQqgMnXHLKtfweF/
            rumi-where-there-is-ruin-there-is-hope-for-a-treasure",
            "title": "Inspiring Quote of the day",
            "background": "https://theysaidso.com/img/bgs/
            man_on_the_mountain.jpg",
            "id": "dPKsui4sQnQqgMnXHLKtfweF"
        }
    ],
    "copyright": "2017-19 theysaidso.com"
    }
}

#extract contents
q = res['contents']['quotes'][0]
q

#output

{'author': 'Rumi',
 'background': 'https://theysaidso.com/img/bgs/man_on_the_mountain.jpg',
 'category': 'inspire',
 'date': '2018-09-29',
 'id': 'dPKsui4sQnQqgMnXHLKtfweF',
 'length': '50',
 'permalink': 'https://theysaidso.com/quote/dPKsui4sQnQqgMnXHLKtfweF/
  rumi-where-there-is-ruin-there-is-hope-for-a-treasure',
 'quote': 'Where there is ruin, there is hope for a treasure.',
 'tags': ['failure', 'inspire', 'learning-from-failure'],
 'title': 'Inspiring Quote of the day'}

#extract only quote
print(q['quote'], '\n--', q['author'])

#output
It wasn't raining when Noah built the ark....
-- Howard Ruff
```

Recipe 1-5. Collecting Data from HTML

HTML is short for *HyperText Markup Language*. It structures webpages and displays them in a browser. There are various HTML tags that build the content. This recipe looks at reading HTML pages.

Problem

You want to read parse/read HTML pages.

Solution

The simplest way is to use the bs4 library.

How It Works

Follow the steps in this section to extract data from the web.

Step 5-1. Install and import all the necessary libraries

First, import the libraries.

```
!pip install bs4
import urllib.request as urllib2
from bs4 import BeautifulSoup
```

Step 5-2. Fetch the HTML file

You can pick any website that you want to extract. Let's use Wikipedia in this example.

```
response = urllib2.urlopen('https://en.wikipedia.org/wiki/
Natural_language_processing')
html_doc = response.read()
```

Step 5-3. Parse the HTML file

Now let's get the data.

```
#Parsing
soup = BeautifulSoup(html_doc, 'html.parser')
# Formating the parsed html file
strhtm = soup.prettify()

# Print few lines
print (strhtm[:1000])

#output

<!DOCTYPE html>
<html class="client-nojs" dir="ltr" lang="en">
 <head>
  <meta charset="utf-8"/>
  <title>
   Natural language processing - Wikipedia
  </title>
  <script>
   document.documentElement.className = document.documentElement.className.
   replace( /(^|\s)client-nojs(\s|$)/, "$1client-js$2" );
  </script>
  <script>
   (window.RLQ=window.RLQ||[]).push(function(){mw.config.set({"wgCanonical
   Namespace":"","wgCanonicalSpecialPageName":false,"wgNamespaceNumber":
   0,"wgPageName":"Natural_language_processing","wgTitle":"Natural language
   processing","wgCurRevisionId":860741853,"wgRevisionId":860741853,
   "wgArticleId":21652,"wgIsArticle":true,"wgIsRedirect":false,"wgAction":
   "view","wgUserName":null,"wgUserGroups":["*"],"wgCategories":["Web
   archive template wayback links","All accuracy disputes","Articles
   with disputed statements from June 2018","Wikipedia articles with
   NDL identifiers","Natural language processing","Computational
   linguistics","Speech recognition","Computational fields of stud
```

11

Step 5-4. Extract a tag value

You can extract a tag's value from the first instance of the tag using the following code.

```
print(soup.title)
print(soup.title.string)
print(soup.a.string)
print(soup.b.string)

#output
 <title>Natural language processing - Wikipedia</title>
Natural language processing - Wikipedia
None
Natural language processing
```

Step 5-5. Extract all instances of a particular tag

Here we get all the instances of the tag that we are interested in.

```
for x in soup.find_all('a'): print(x.string)

#sample output
 None
Jump to navigation
Jump to search
Language processing in the brain
None
None
automated online assistant
customer service
[1]
computer science
artificial intelligence
natural language
speech recognition
natural language understanding
natural language generation
```

Step 5-6. Extract all text from a particular tag

Finally, we get the text.

```
for x in soup.find_all('p'): print(x.text)
```

```
#sample output
Natural language processing (NLP) is an area of computer science and
artificial intelligence concerned with the interactions between computers
and human (natural) languages, in particular how to program computers to
process and analyze large amounts of natural language data.

Challenges in natural language processing frequently involve speech
recognition, natural language understanding, and natural language
generation.

The history of natural language processing generally started in the 1950s,
although work can be found from earlier periods.
In 1950, Alan Turing published an article titled "Intelligence" which
proposed what is now called the Turing test as a criterion of intelligence.
```

Note that the p tag extracted most of the text on the page.

Recipe 1-6. Parsing Text Using Regular Expressions

This recipe discusses how regular expressions are helpful when dealing with text data. Regular expressions are required when dealing with raw data from the web that contains HTML tags, long text, and repeated text. During the process of developing your application, as well as in output, you don't need such data.

You can do allsorts of basic and advanced data cleaning using regular expressions.

Problem

You want to parse text data using regular expressions.

Solution

The best way is to use the re library in Python.

How It Works

Let's look at some of the ways we can use regular expressions for our tasks.

The basic flags are I, L, M, S, U, X.

- `re.I` ignores casing.

- `re.L` finds a local dependent.

- `re.M` finds patterns throughout multiple lines.

- `re.S` finds dot matches.

- `re.U` works for Unicode data.

- `re.X` writes regex in a more readable format.

The following describes regular expressions' functionalities.

- Find a single occurrence of characters a and b: `[ab]`

- Find characters except for a and b: `[^ab]`

- Find the character range of a to z: `[a-z]`

- Find a character range except a to z: `[^a-z]`

- Find all the characters from both a to z and A to Z: `[a-zA-Z]`

- Find any single character: `[]`

- Find any whitespace character: `\s`

- Find any non-whitespace character: `\S`

- Find any digit: `\d`

- Find any non-digit: `\D`

- Find any non-words: `\W`

- Find any words: `\w`

- Find either a or b: `(a|b)`

- The occurrence of a is either zero or one

  - Matches zero or not more than one occurrence: `a?` ; `?`

  - The occurrence of a is zero or more times: `a*` ; `*` matches zero or more than that

- The occurrence of a is one or more times: `a+` ; `+ matches occurrences one or more than one time`

- Match three simultaneous occurrences of a: `a{3}`

- Match three or more simultaneous occurrences of a: `a{3,}`

- Match three to six simultaneous occurrences of a: `a{3,6}`

- Start of a string: `^`

- End of a string: `$`

- Match word boundary: `\b`

- Non-word boundary: `\B`

The `re.match()` and `re.search()` functions find patterns, which are then processed according to the requirements of the application.

Let's look at the differences between `re.match()` and `re.search()`.

- `re.match()` checks for a match only at the beginning of the string. So, if it finds a pattern at the beginning of the input string, it returns the matched pattern; otherwise, it returns a noun.

- `re.search()` checks for a match anywhere in the string. It finds all the occurrences of the pattern in the given input string or data.

Now let's look at a few examples using these regular expressions.

Tokenizing

Tokenizing means splitting a sentence into words. One way to do this is to use `re.split`.

```
# Import library

import re

#run the split query

re.split('\s+','I like this book.')

['I', 'like', 'this', 'book.']
```

For an explanation of regex, please refer to the main recipe.

Extracting Email IDs

The simplest way to extract email IDs is to use `re.findall`.

1. Read/create the document or sentences.

   ```
   doc = "For more details please mail us at: xyz@abc.com, pqr@mno.com"
   ```

2. Execute the `re.findall` function.

   ```
   addresses = re.findall(r'[\w\.-]+@[\w\.-]+', doc)
   for address in addresses.
       print(address)

   #Output
   xyz@abc.com
   pqr@mno.com
   ```

Replacing Email IDs

Let's replace email IDs in sentences or documents with other email IDs. The simplest way to do this is by using `re.sub`.

1. Read/create the document or sentences.

   ```
   doc = "For more details please mail us at xyz@abc.com"
   ```

2. Execute the `re.sub` function.

   ```
   new_email_address = re.sub(r'([\w\.-]+)@([\w\.-]+)',
   r'pqr@mno.com', doc)
   print(new_email_address)

   #Output
   For more details please mail us at pqr@mno.com
   ```

For an explanation of regex, please refer to Recipe 1-6.

If you observe in both instances when dealing with email using regex, we have implemented a very basic one. We state that words separated by @ help capture email IDs. However, there could be many edge cases; for example, the dot (`.`) incorporates domain names and handles numbers, the + (plus sign), and so on, because they can be part of an email ID.

The following is an advanced regex to extract/find/replace email IDs.

([a-zA-Z0-9+._-]+@[a-zA-Z0-9._-]+\.[a-zA-Z0-9_-]+)

There are even more complex ones to handle all the edge cases (e.g., ".co.in" email IDs). Please give it a try.

Extracting Data from an eBook and Performing regex

Let's solve a case study that extracts data from an ebook by using the techniques you have learned so far.

1. Extract the content from the book.

    ```python
    # Import library

    import re
    import requests

    #url you want to extract
    url = 'https://www.gutenberg.org/files/2638/2638-0.txt'

    #function to extract
    def get_book(url).
     # Sends a http request to get the text from project Gutenberg
     raw = requests.get(url).text
     # Discards the metadata from the beginning of the book
     start = re.search(r"\*\*\* START OF THIS PROJECT GUTENBERG EBOOK
     .* \*\*\*",raw ).end()
     # Discards the metadata from the end of the book
     stop = re.search(r"II", raw).start()
     # Keeps the relevant text
     text = raw[start:stop]
     return text

    # processing
    def preprocess(sentence).
     return re.sub('[^A-Za-z0-9.]+' , ' ', sentence).lower()

    #calling the above function
    ```

```
book = get_book(url)
processed_book = preprocess(book)
print(processed_book)

# Output
  produced by martin adamson david widger with corrections by andrew
  sly the idiot by fyodor dostoyevsky translated by eva martin
  part i i. towards the end of november during a thaw at nine o
  clock one morning a train on the warsaw and petersburg railway
  was approaching the latter city at full speed. the morning was so
  damp and misty that it was only with great difficulty that the day
  succeeded in breaking and it was impossible to distinguish anything
  more than a few yards away from the carriage windows. some of the
  passengers by this particular train were returning from abroad
  but the third class carriages were the best filled chiefly with
  insignificant persons of various occupations and degrees picked up
  at the different stations nearer town. all of them seemed weary and
  most of them had sleepy eyes and a shivering expression while their
  complexions generally appeared to have taken on the colour of the
  fog outside. when da
```

2. Perform an exploratory data analysis on this data using regex.

```
# Count number of times "the" is appeared in the book
len(re.findall(r'the', processed_book))
```

```
#Output
302
```

```
#Replace "i" with "I"
processed_book = re.sub(r'\si\s', " I ", processed_book)
print(processed_book)
```

```
#output
  produced by martin adamson david widger with corrections by
  andrew sly the idiot by fyodor dostoyevsky translated by eva
  martin part I i. towards the end of november during a thaw at
  nine o clock one morning a train on the warsaw and petersburg
```

railway was approaching the latter city at full speed. the morning was so damp and misty that it was only with great difficulty that the day succeeded in breaking and it was impossible to distinguish anything more than a few yards away from the carriage windows. some of the passengers by this particular train were returning from abroad but the third class carriages were the best filled chiefly with insignificant persons of various occupations and degrees picked up at the different stations nearer town. all of them seemed weary and most of them had sleepy eyes and a shivering expression while their complexions generally appeared to have taken on the colour of the fog outside. when da

```
#find all occurance of text in the format "abc--xyz"
re.findall(r'[a-zA-Z0-9]*--[a-zA-Z0-9]*', book)
```

```
#output
['ironical--it',
 'malicious--smile',
 'fur--or',
 'astrachan--overcoat',
 'it--the',
 'Italy--was',
 'malady--a',
 'money--and',
 'little--to',
 'No--Mr',
 'is--where',
 'I--I',
 'I--',
 '--though',
 'crime--we',
 'or--judge',
 'gaiters--still',
 '--if',
 'through--well',
 'say--through',
```

```
'however--and',
'Epanchin--oh',
'too--at',
'was--and',
'Andreevitch--that',
'everyone--that',
'reduce--or',
'raise--to',
'listen--and',
'history--but',
'individual--one',
'yes--I',
'but--',
't--not',
'me--then',
'perhaps--',
'Yes--those',
'me--is',
'servility--if',
'Rogojin--hereditary',
'citizen--who',
'least--goodness',
'memory--but',
'latter--since',
'Rogojin--hung',
'him--I',
'anything--she',
'old--and',
'you--scarecrow',
'certainly--certainly',
'father--I',
'Barashkoff--I',
'see--and',
'everything--Lebedeff',
'about--he',
```

```
  'now--I',
  'Lihachof--',
  'Zaleshoff--looking',
  'old--fifty',
  'so--and',
  'this--do',
  'day--not',
  'that--',
  'do--by',
  'know--my',
  'illness--I',
  'well--here',
  'fellow--you']
```

Recipe 1-7. Handling Strings

This recipe discusses how to handle strings and deal with textual data. You can do all sorts of basic text explorations using string operations.

Problem

You want to explore handling strings.

Solution

The simplest way is to use the following string functionality.

- s.find(t) is an index of the first instance of string t inside s (-1 if not found)

- s.rfind(t) is an index of the last instance of string t inside s (-1 if not found)

- s.index(t) is like s.find(t) except it raises ValueError if not found

- s.rindex(t) is like s.rfind(t) except it raises ValueError if not found

- s.join(text) combines the words of the text into a string using s as the glue

- `s.split(t)` splits s into a list wherever a t is found (whitespace by default)

- `s.splitlines()` splits s into a list of strings, one per line

- `s.lower()` is a lowercase version of the string s

- `s.upper()` is an uppercase version of the string s

- `s.title()` is a titlecased version of the string s

- `s.strip()` is a copy of s without leading or trailing whitespace

- `s.replace(t, u)` replaces instances of t with u inside s

How It Works

Now let's look at a few of the examples.

Replacing Content

Create a string and replace the content. Creating strings is easy. It is done by enclosing the characters in single or double quotes. And to replace, you can use the `replace` function.

1. Create a string.

   ```
   String_v1 = "I am exploring NLP"

   #To extract particular character or range of characters from string

   print(String_v1[0])

   #output
   "I"

   #To extract the word "exploring"

   print(String_v1[5:14])

   #output
   exploring
   ```

2. Replace "exploring" with "learning" in the preceding string.

```
String_v2 = String_v1.replace("exploring", "learning")
print(String_v2)
```

```
#Output
I am learning NLP
```

Concatenating Two Strings

The following is simple code.

```
s1 = "nlp"
s2 = "machine learning"
s3 = s1+s2
print(s3)
```

```
#output
'nlpmachine learning'
```

Searching for a Substring in a String

Use the find function to fetch the starting index value of the substring in the whole string.

```
var="I am learning NLP"
f= "learn"
var.find(f)
```

```
#output
5
```

Recipe 1-8. Scraping Text from the Web

This recipe discusses how to scrape data from the web.

Caution   Before scraping any websites, blogs, or ecommerce sites, please make sure you read the site's terms and conditions on whether it gives permissions for data scraping. Generally, robots.txt contains the terms and conditions (e.g., see `www.alixpartners.com/robots.txt`) and a site map contains a URL's map (e.g., see `www.alixpartners.com/sitemap.xml`).

Web scraping is also known as web harvesting and web data extraction. It is a technique to extract a large amount of data from websites and save it in a database or locally. You can use this data to extract information related to your customers, users, or products for the business's benefit.

A basic understanding of HTML is a prerequisite.

Problem

You want to extract data from the web by scraping. Let's use IMDB.com as an example of scraping top movies.

Solution

The simplest way to do this is by using Python's Beautiful Soup or Scrapy libraries. Let's use Beautiful Soup in this recipe.

How It Works

Follow the steps in this section to extract data from the web.

Step 8-1. Install all the necessary libraries

```
!pip install bs4
!pip install requests
```

Step 8-2. Import the libraries

```
from bs4 import BeautifulSoup
import requests
import pandas as pd
from pandas import Series, DataFrame
from ipywidgets import FloatProgress
from time import sleep
from IPython.display import display
import re
import pickle
```

Step 8-3. Identify the URL to extract the data

```
url = 'http://www.imdb.com/chart/top?ref_=nv_mv_250_6'
```

Step 8-4. Request the URL and download the content using Beautiful Soup

```
result = requests.get(url)
c = result.content
soup = BeautifulSoup(c,"lxml")
```

Step 8-5. Understand the website's structure to extract the required information

Go to the website and right-click the page content to inspect the site's HTML structure.

Identify the data and fields that you want to extract. For example, you want the movie name and IMDB rating.

Check which div or class in the HTML contains the movie names and parse the Beautiful Soup accordingly. In this example, you can parse the soup through `<table class ="chart full-width">` and `<td class="titleColumn">` to extract the movie name.

Similarly, you can fetch other data; refer to the code in step 8-6.

```
▼<table class="chart full-width" data-caller-name="chart-
top250movie">
  ▶<colgroup>…</colgroup>
  ▶<thead>…</thead>
  ▼<tbody class="lister-list">
    ▼<tr>
      ▶<td class="posterColumn">…</td>
      ▶<td class="titleColumn">…</td> == $0
      ▶<td class="ratingColumn imdbRating">…</td>
      ▶<td class="ratingColumn">…</td>
```

Step 8-6. Use Beautiful Soup to extract and parse the data from HTML tags

```python
summary = soup.find('div',{'class':'article'})

# Create empty lists to append the extracted data.

moviename = []
cast = []
description = []
rating = []
ratingoutof = []
year = []
genre = []
movielength = []
rot_audscore = []
rot_avgrating = []
rot_users = []

# Extracting the required data from the html soup.

rgx = re.compile('[%s]' % '()')
f = FloatProgress(min=0, max=250)
display(f)
for row,i in zip(summary.find('table').findAll('tr'),range(len(summary.
find('table').findAll('tr')))):
```

```
for sitem in row.findAll('span',{'class':'secondaryInfo'}).
    s = sitem.find(text=True)
    year.append(rgx.sub(", s))
for ritem in row.findAll('td',{'class':'ratingColumn imdbRating'}).
    for iget in ritem.findAll('strong').
        rating.append(iget.find(text=True))
        ratingoutof.append(iget.get('title').split(' ', 4)[3])
for item in row.findAll('td',{'class':'titleColumn'}).
    for href in item.findAll('a',href=True).
        moviename.append(href.find(text=True))
        rurl = 'https://www.rottentomatoes.com/m/'+ href.
        find(text=True)
        try.
            rresult = requests.get(rurl)
        except requests.exceptions.ConnectionError.
            status_code = "Connection refused"
        rc = rresult.content
        rsoup = BeautifulSoup(rc)
        try:
            rot_audscore.append(rsoup.find('div',{'class':'meter-
            value'}).find('span',{'class':'superPageFontColor'}).text)
            rot_avgrating.append(rsoup.find('div',{'class':'audience-
            info hidden-xs superPageFontColor'}).find('div').
            contents[2].strip())
            rot_users.append(rsoup.find('div',{'class':'audience-info
            hidden-xs superPageFontColor'}).contents[3].contents[2].
            strip())
        except AttributeError.
            rot_audscore.append("")
            rot_avgrating.append("")
            rot_users.append("")
        cast.append(href.get('title'))
        imdb = "http://www.imdb.com" + href.get('href')
```

```
        try.
            iresult = requests.get(imdb)
            ic = iresult.content
            isoup = BeautifulSoup(ic)
            description.append(isoup.find('div',{'class':
            'summary_text'}).find(text=True).strip())
            genre.append(isoup.find('span',{'class':'itemprop'}).
            find(text=True))
            movielength.append(isoup.find('time',{'itemprop':'durati
            on'}).find(text=True).strip())
        except requests.exceptions.ConnectionError.
            description.append("")
            genre.append("")
            movielength.append("")
    sleep(.1)
    f.value = i
```

Note that there is a high chance that you might encounter an error while executing this script because of the following reasons.

- Your request to the URL fails. If so, try again after some time. This is common in web scraping.

- The webpages are dynamic, which means the HTML tags keep changing. Study the tags and make small changes in the code in accordance with HTML, and you should be good to go.

Step 8-7. Convert lists to a data frame and perform an analysis that meets business requirements

```
# List to pandas series

moviename = Series(moviename)
cast = Series(cast)
description = Series(description)
rating = Series(rating)
ratingoutof = Series(ratingoutof)
year = Series(year)
```

```
genre = Series(genre)
movielength = Series(movielength)
rot_audscore = Series(rot_audscore)
rot_avgrating = Series(rot_avgrating)
rot_users = Series(rot_users)

# creating dataframe and doing analysis

imdb_df = pd.concat([moviename,year,description,genre,movielength,cast,
          rating,ratingoutof,rot_audscore,rot_avgrating,rot_users],axis=1)
imdb_df.columns = ['moviename','year','description','genre','movielength',
                'cast','imdb_rating','imdb_ratingbasedon',
                'tomatoes_audscore','tomatoes_rating',
                'tomatoes_ratingbasedon']
imdb_df['rank'] = imdb_df.index + 1
imdb_df.head(1)
```

#output

	moviename	year	description	genre	movielength	cast	imdb_rating	imdb_ratingbasedon
0	The Shawshank Redemption	1994	Two imprisoned men bond over a number of years...	wrongful imprisonment	NaN	Frank Darabont (dir.), Tim Robbins, Morgan Fre...	9.2	1,994,354

Step 8-8. Download the data frame

```
# Saving the file as CSV.
```

```
imdb_df.to_csv("imdbdataexport.csv")
```

This chapter implemented most of the techniques to extract text data from sources. In the coming chapters, you look at how to explore, process, and clean data. You also learn about feature engineering and building NLP applications.

CHAPTER 2

Exploring and Processing Text Data

This chapter discusses various methods and techniques to preprocess textual data and exploratory data analysis. It covers the following recipes.

Recipe 1. Lowercasing

Recipe 2. Punctuation removal

Recipe 3. Stop words removal

Recipe 4. Text standardization

Recipe 5. Spelling correction

Recipe 6. Tokenization

Recipe 7. Stemming

Recipe 8. Lemmatization

Recipe 9. Exploratory data analysis

Recipe 10. Dealing with emojis and emoticons

Recipe 11. End-to-end processing pipeline

Before directly jumping into the recipes, let's first understand the need for preprocessing the text data. As you know, about 90% of the world's data is unstructured and may be present in the form of an image, text, audio, and video. Text can come in various forms, from a list of individual words to sentences to multiple paragraphs with special characters (like tweets and other punctuations). It also may be present in the form of web, HTML, documents, and so on. And this data is never clean and consists of a lot of noise. It needs to be treated and then perform a few preprocessing functions to

© Akshay Kulkarni and Adarsha Shivananda 2021
A. Kulkarni and A. Shivananda, *Natural Language Processing Recipes*,
https://doi.org/10.1007/978-1-4842-7351-7_2

make sure you have the right input data for the feature engineering and model building. If you don't preprocess the data, any algorithms built on top of such data do not add any value to a business. This reminds us of a very popular phrase in data science: "Garbage in, garbage out."

Preprocessing involves transforming raw text data into an understandable format. Real-world data is often incomplete, inconsistent, and filled with a lot of noise, and is likely to contain many errors. Preprocessing is a proven method of resolving such issues. Data preprocessing prepares raw text data for further processing.

Recipe 2-1. Converting Text Data to Lowercase

This recipe discusses how to lowercase the text data to have all the data in a uniform format and make sure "NLP" and "nlp" are treated as the same.

Problem

You want to lowercase the text data.

Solution

The simplest way is to use the default lower() function in Python.

The lower() method converts all uppercase characters in a string to lowercase characters and returns them.

How It Works

Follow the steps in this section to lowercase a given text or document. Here, Python is used.

Step 1-1. Read/create the text data

Let's create a list of strings and assign it to a variable.

```
text=['This is introduction to NLP','It is likely to be useful, to people ',
'Machine learning is the new electrcity','There would be less hype around
AI and more action going forward','python is the best tool!','R is good
langauage','I like this book','I want more books like this']
```

```
#convert list to data frame
import pandas as pd
df = pd.DataFrame({'tweet':text})
print(df)

#output

                                                   tweet
0                         This is introduction to NLP
1                  It is likely to be useful, to people
2                    Machine learning is the new electrcity
3   There would be less hype around AI and more ac...
4                              python is the best tool!
5                                 R is good langauage
6                                    I like this book
7                          I want more books like this
```

Step 1-2. Execute the lower() function on the text data

When there is only a string, directly apply the lower() function as follows.

```
x = 'Testing'
x2 = x.lower()
print(x2)

#output
'testing'
```

When you want to perform lowercasing on a data frame, use the apply function as follows.

```
df['tweet'] = df['tweet'].apply(lambda x: " ".join(x.lower() for x in
x.split()))
df['tweet']

#output
0                          this is introduction to nlp
1                  it is likely to be useful, to people
2                    machine learning is the new electrcity
3       there would be less hype around ai and more ac...
```

```
4                            python is the best tool!
5                               r is good langauage
6                                  i like this book
7                        i want more books like this
```

Alternatively, you can use the following code:

```
df['tweet'] = df['tweet'].str.lower()
```

That's all. The entire tweet column was converted to lowercase. Let's see what else you can do in the next recipes.

Recipe 2-2. Removing Punctuation

This recipe discusses how to remove punctuation from text data. This step is very important since punctuation doesn't add any extra information or value. Hence removal of all such instances reduces the size of the data and increases computational efficiency.

Problem

You want to remove punctuation from the text data.

Solution

The simplest way is to use regex and the `replace()` function in Python.

How It Works

Follow the steps in this section to remove punctuation from the text data.

Step 2-1. Read/create the text data

Let's create a list of strings and assign it to a variable.

```
text=['This is introduction to NLP','It is likely to be useful, to people ',
'Machine learning is the new electrcity','There would be less hype around
AI and more action going forward','python is the best tool!','R is good
langauage','I like this book','I want more books like this']
```

```
#convert list to dataframe
import pandas as pd
df = pd.DataFrame({'tweet':text})
print(df)
#output
 tweet
0 This is introduction to NLP
1 It is likely to be useful, to people
2 Machine learning is the new electrcity
3 There would be less hype around AI and more ac...
4 python is the best tool!
5 R is good langauage
6 I like this book
7 I want more books like this
```

Step 2-2. Execute the replace() function on the text data

With the regex and replace() function, you can remove punctuation as follows.

```
import re

s = "I. like. This book!"
s1 = re.sub(r'[^\w\s]',",s)
s1

#output
'I like This book'
```

    Or:

```
df['tweet'] = df['tweet'].str.replace('[^\w\s]',")
df['tweet']

#output
0                    this is introduction to nlp
1               it is likely to be useful to people
2               machine learning is the new electrcity
3     there would be less hype around ai and more ac...
4                         python is the best tool
```

```
5                                  r is good langauage
6                                    i like this book
7                          i want more books like this
```

Or:

```
import string

s = "I. like. This book!"

for c in string.punctuation:
    s= s.replace(c,"")
s

#output
'I like This book'
```

Recipe 2-3. Removing Stop Words

This recipe discusses how to remove stop words. Stop words are very common words that carry no meaning or less meaning compared to other keywords. If you remove the less commonly used words, you can focus on the important keywords. For example, in a search engine, if your search query is "How to develop a chatbot using Python," if the search engine tries to find webpages that contain the words *how*, *to*, *develop*, *chatbot*, *using*, and *python*, the search engine finds many more pages that contain *how* and *to* than pages that contain information about developing a chatbot because the words *how* and *to* are so commonly used in the English language. So, if you remove such words, the search engine can focus on retrieving pages that contain the keywords *develop*, *chatbot*, and *python*, which would more closely bring up pages that are of real interest. Similarly, you can also remove other common words and rare words.

Problem

You want to remove stop words.

Solution

The simplest way is to use the NLTK library or build your own stop words file.

How It Works

Follow the steps in this section to remove stop words from the text data.

Step 3-1. Read/create the text data

Let's create a list of strings and assign it to a variable.

```
text=['This is introduction to NLP','It is likely to be useful, to people ',
'Machine learning is the new electrcity','There would be less hype around
AI and more action going forward','python is the best tool!','R is good
langauage','I like this book','I want more books like this']
```

```
#convert list to data frame
import pandas as pd
df = pd.DataFrame({'tweet':text})
print(df)
```

```
#output
 tweet
0 This is introduction to NLP
1 It is likely to be useful, to people
2 Machine learning is the new electrcity
3 There would be less hype around AI and more ac...
4 python is the best tool!
5 R is good langauage
6 I like this book
7 I want more books like this
```

Step 3-2. Remove punctuation from the text data

With the NLTK library, you can remove punctuation, as shown next.

```
#install and import libraries
```

```
!pip install nltk
import nltk
nltk.download()
from nltk.corpus import stopwords
```

```
#remove stop words

stop = stopwords.words('english')
df['tweet'] = df['tweet'].apply(lambda x: "
            ".join(x for x in x.split() if x not in stop))
df['tweet']

#output
```

```
0                        introduction nlp
1                     likely useful people
2               machine learning new electrcity
3   would less hype around ai action going forward
4                       python best tool
5                       r good langauage
6                            like book
7                       want books like
```

There are no stop words now. Everything has been removed in this step.

Recipe 2-4. Standardizing Text

This recipe discusses how to standardize text. But before that, let's discuss text standardization and why you need it. Most textual data is in customer reviews, blogs, or tweets, where there is a high chance of people using short words and abbreviations to represent the same meaning. This may help the downstream process to easily understand and resolve the semantics of the text.

Problem

You want to standardize text.

Solution

You can write your own custom dictionary to look for short words and abbreviations. First, you need to see if there are any short words and abbreviations present in the data. That can be achieved by looking at the frequency distribution of words in our document or visualizing through word cloud before creating a custom dictionary.

How It Works

Follow the steps in this section to perform text standardization.

Step 4-1. Create a custom lookup dictionary

The dictionary is for text standardization based on your data.

```
lookup_dict = {'nlp':'natural language processing', 'ur':'your',
"wbu" : "what about you"}
```

```
import re
```

Step 4-2. Create a custom function for text standardization

Here is the code:

```
def text_std(input_text):
 words = input_text.split()
 new_words = []
 for word in words:
     word = re.sub(r'[^\w\s]','',word)
     if word.lower() in lookup_dict:
         word = lookup_dict[word.lower()]
         new_words.append(word)
         new_text = " ".join(new_words)
 return new_text
```

Step 4-3. Run the text_std function

The output also needs to be checked.

```
text_std("I like nlp it's ur choice")
```

```
#output
'natural language processing your'
```

Here, nlp has standardized to 'natural language processing' and ur to 'your'.

Recipe 2-5. Correcting Spelling

This recipe discusses how to do spelling correction. But before that, let's look at why this spelling correction is important. Most text data is in customer reviews, blogs, or tweets, where there is a high chance of people using short words and making typo errors. This reduces multiple copies of words, which represent the same meaning. For example, "proccessing" and "processing" are treated as different words even if used in the same sense.

Note that abbreviations should be handled before this step, or else the corrector would fail at times. Say, for example, "ur" (actually means "your") would be corrected to "or."

Problem

You want to do spelling correction.

Solution

The simplest way is to use the TextBlob library.

How It Works

Follow the steps in this section to make spelling corrections.

Step 5-1. Read/create the text data

Let's create a list of strings and assign it to a variable.

```
text=['Introduction to NLP','It is likely to be useful, to people
','Machine learning is the new electrcity', 'R is good langauage','I like
this book','I want more books like this']
```

```
#convert list to dataframe
import pandas as pd
df = pd.DataFrame({'tweet':text})
print(df)
```

```
#output

                                    tweet
0                       Introduction to NLP
1      It is likely to be useful, to people
2   Machine learning is the new electrcity
3                       R is good langauage
4                          I like this book
5              I want more books like this
```

Step 5-2. Execute spelling correction on the text data

Using TextBlob, you can do spelling, as shown next.

```
#Install textblob library
!pip install textblob
```

```
#import libraries and use 'correct' function
```

```
from textblob import TextBlob
```

```
df['tweet'].apply(lambda x: str(TextBlob(x).correct()))
```

```
#output
0                       Introduction to NLP
1      It is likely to be useful, to people
2   Machine learning is the new electricity
3                        R is good language
4                          I like this book
5              I want more books like this
```

Note that the spelling of electricity and language were corrected.

```
#You can also use autocorrect library as shown below
```

```
#install autocorrect
```

```
!pip install autocorrect
```

```
from autocorrect import spell
print(spell(u'mussage'))
print(spell(u'sirvice'))

#output
'message'
'service'
```

Recipe 2-6. Tokenizing Text

This recipe looks at ways to tokenize. Tokenization refers to splitting text into minimal meaningful units. There is a sentence tokenizer and a word tokenizer. You see a word tokenizer in this recipe. It is a mandatory step in text preprocessing for any kind of analysis. There are many libraries to perform tokenization like NLTK, spaCy, and TextBlob. Here are a few ways to achieve it.

Problem

You want to do tokenization.

Solution

The simplest way is to use the TextBlob library.

How It Works

Follow the steps in this section to perform tokenization.

Step 6-1. Read/create the text data

Let's create a list of strings and assign it to a variable.

```
text=['This is introduction to NLP','It is likely to be useful, to people ',
'Machine learning is the new electrcity','There would be less hype around
AI and more action going forward','python is the best tool!','R is good
langauage','I like this book','I want more books like this']
```

```
#convert list to dataframe
import pandas as pd
df = pd.DataFrame({'tweet':text})
print(df)
```

```
#output
 tweet
0 This is introduction to NLP
1 It is likely to be useful, to people
2 Machine learning is the new electrcity
3 There would be less hype around AI and more ac...
4 python is the best tool!
5 R is good langauage
6 I like this book
7 I want more books like this
```

Step 6-2. Tokenize the text data

The result of tokenization is a list of tokens.

```
#Using textblob
from textblob import TextBlob
TextBlob(df['tweet'][3]).words
```

```
#output
WordList(['would', 'less', 'hype', 'around', 'ai', 'action', 'going',
'forward'])
```

```
#using NLTK
import nltk
```

```
#create data
mystring = "My favorite animal is cat"
```

```
nltk.word_tokenize(mystring)
```

```
#output
['My', 'favorite', 'animal', 'is', 'cat']
```

```
#using split function from python
mystring.split()
```

```
#output
['My', 'favorite', 'animal', 'is', 'cat']
```

Recipe 2-7. Stemming

This recipe discusses stemming. Stemming is the process of extracting a root word. For example, *fish*, *fishes*, and *fishing* are stemmed into *fish*.

Problem

You want to do stemming.

Solution

The simplest way is to use NLTK or the TextBlob library.

How It Works

Follow the steps in this section to perform stemming.

Step 7-1. Read the text data

Let's create a list of strings and assign it to a variable.

```
text=['I like fishing','I eat fish','There are many fishes in pound']
```

```
#convert list to dataframe
import pandas as pd
df = pd.DataFrame({'tweet':text})
print(df)
```

```
#output
```

```
                                    tweet
0                          I like fishing
1                              I eat fish
2      There are many fishes in pound
```

Step 7-2. Stem the text

Execute the following code on the text data.

```
#Import library
from nltk.stem import PorterStemmer

st = PorterStemmer()

df['tweet'][:5].apply(lambda x: " ".join([st.stem(word) for word in
x.split()]))
```

```
#output
0                              I like fish
1                               I eat fish
2        there are mani fish in pound
```

Note that fish, fishing, and fishes have all been stemmed to fish.

Recipe 2-8. Lemmatizing

This recipe discusses lemmatization, the process of extracting a root word by considering the vocabulary. For example, *good*, *better*, or *best* is lemmatized into *good*.

The part of speech of a word is determined in lemmatization. It returns the dictionary form of a word, which must be valid. While stemming just extracts the root word.

- Lemmatization handles matching *car* to *cars* along with matching *car* to *automobile*.

- Stemming handles matching *car* to *cars*.

Lemmatization can get better results.

- The stemmed form of *leafs* is *leaf*.

- The stemmed form of *leaves* is *leav*.

- The lemmatized form of *leafs* is *leaf*.

- The lemmatized form of *leaves* is *leaf*.

Problem

You want to perform lemmatization.

Solution

The simplest way is to use NLTK or the TextBlob library.

How It Works

Follow the steps in this section to perform lemmatization.

Step 8-1. Read the text data

Let's create a list of strings and assign it to a variable.

```
text=['I like fishing','I eat fish','There are many fishes in pound',
'leaves and leaf']

#convert list to dataframe
import pandas as pd
df = pd.DataFrame({'tweet':text})

print(df)
                              tweet
0                   I like fishing
1                       I eat fish
2   There are multiple fishes in pound
3                   leaves and leaf
```

Step 8-2. Lemmatize the data

Execute the following code on the text data.

```
#Import library
from textblob import Word

#Code for lemmatize
df['tweet'] = df['tweet'].apply(lambda x: " ".join([Word(word).lemmatize()
for word in x.split()]))

df['tweet']

#output
0                    I like fishing
1                       I eat fish
2    There are multiple fish in pound
3                    leaf and leaf
```

You can observe that fish and fishes are lemmatized to fish, and leaves and leaf are lemmatized to leaf.

Recipe 2-9. Exploring Text Data

So far, you should be comfortable with data collection and text preprocessing. Let's perform some exploratory data analysis.

Problem

You want to explore and understand the text data.

Solution

The simplest way is to use NLTK or the TextBlob library.

How It Works

Follow the steps in this process.

Step 9-1. Read the text data

Execute the following code to download the dataset, if you haven't already done so.

```
nltk.download().
#Importing data
import nltk
from nltk.corpus import webtext
nltk.download('webtext')
wt_sentences = webtext.sents('firefox.txt')
wt_words = webtext.words('firefox.txt')
```

Step 9-2. Import necessary libraries

Import Library for computing frequency:

```
from nltk.probability import FreqDist
from nltk.corpus import stopwords
import string
```

Step 9-3 Check the number of words in the data

Count the number of words:

```
len(wt_sentences)
```

```
#output
1142
```

```
len(wt_words)
```

```
#output
102457
```

Step 9-4. Compute the frequency of all words in the reviews

Generating frequency for all the words:

```
frequency_dist = nltk.FreqDist(wt_words)
frequency_dist

#showing only top few results

FreqDist({'slowing': 1,
          'warnings': 6,
          'rule': 1,
          'Top': 2,
          'XBL': 12,
          'installation': 44,
          'Networking': 1,
          'inccorrect': 1,
          'killed': 3,
          ']"': 1,
          'LOCKS': 1,
          'limited': 2,
          'cookies': 57,
          'method': 12,
          'arbitrary': 2,
          'b': 3,
          'titlebar': 6,

sorted_frequency_dist =sorted(frequency_dist,key=frequency_dist.__getitem__,
reverse=True)
sorted_frequency_dist
['.',
 'in',
 'to',
 '"',
 'the',
 "'",
 'not',
```

```
'-',
'when',
'on',
'a',
'is',
't',
'and',
'of',
```

Step 9-5. Consider words with length greater than 3 and plot

Let's only consider words if their frequency is greater than three.

```
large_words = dict([(k,v) for k,v in frequency_dist.items() if len(k)>3])
```

```
frequency_dist = nltk.FreqDist(large_words)
frequency_dist.plot(50,cumulative=False)
```

#output

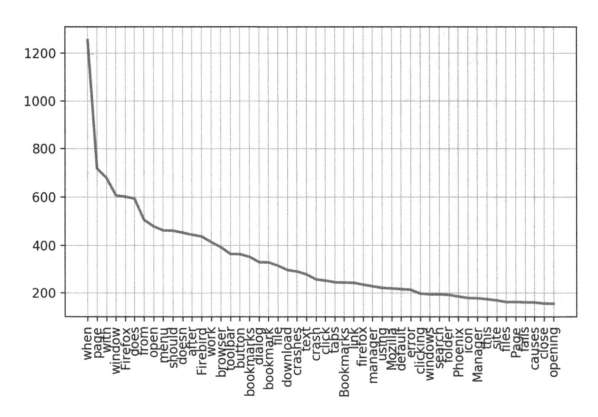

Step 9-6. Build a word cloud

A word cloud is a pictorial representation of the most frequently repeated words.

```
#install library
!pip install wordcloud
```

```
#build wordcloud
```

```
from wordcloud import WordCloud
wcloud = WordCloud().generate_from_frequencies(frequency_dist)
```

```
#plotting the wordcloud
```

```
import matplotlib.pyplot as plt
plt.imshow(wcloud, interpolation="bilinear")
plt.axis("off")
(-0.5, 399.5, 199.5, -0.5)
plt.show()
```

```
#output
```

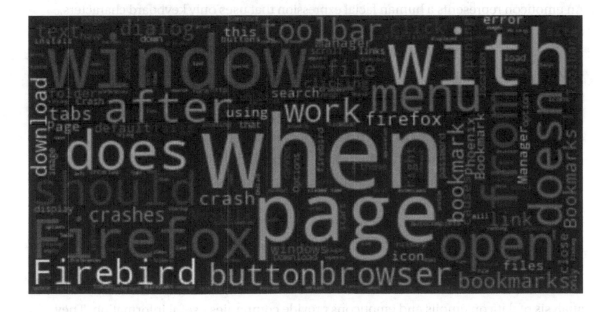

Next, let's remove the stop wordsand then build the word cloud. The output should look something like what's shown in the next recipe.

Recipe 2-10. Dealing with Emojis and Emoticons

What is an emoji? The word *emoji* essentially means "image character" (from the Japanese *e* meaning "image: and *moji* meaning "letter character"). What is an emoticon? :): -]
An emoticon represents a human facial expression that uses only keyboard characters, such as letters, numbers, and punctuation marks.

In today's online world, emojis and emoticons are the primary language that allows us to communicate with anyone globally when we need to be fast and accurate. Both emoji and emoticons play an essential role in text analysis. They are used most frequently in social media, emails, and text messages, although they can be found in any type of electronic communication. In cases where emotions are not useful, you may need to remove them from your textual analysis. On the other hand, you should retain them because they provide valuable information, especially in sentiment analysis, and removing them might not be an adequate solution; for example, if a company wants to know how people feel about a new product, a new campaign, or the brand on social media.

Emojis help identify where consumer engagement needs to be improved by imagining users' moods, attitudes, and opinions. This provides essential information, and it is vital for any business to better understand their customers' feelings. The collection and analysis of data on emojis and emoticons provide companies useful information. They can be converted into a word format to be used in modeling processes. In this book, you see how to save emoji and emoticons in word form using Python.

This book uses a library called emot.

Problem

You want to replace an emoji with a relevant, meaningful word.

Solution

The simplest way is to use the emot library.

How It Works

Follow these next steps.

Step 10-A1. Read the text data

```
#create sample text data with emoji
text1 = "What are you saying 😂. I am the boss😎, and why are you so 😒"
```

Step 10-A2. Install and import necessary libraries

```
#Installing emot library
!pip install emot

#Importing libraries
import re
from emot.emo_unicode import UNICODE_EMO, EMOTICONS
```

Step 10-A3. Write a function that coverts emojis into words

```
# Function for converting emojis into word
def converting_emojis(text):
    for emot in UNICODE_EMO:
        text = text.replace(emot, "_".join(UNICODE_EMO[emot].
        replace(",","").replace(":","").split()))
    return text
```

Step 10-A4. Pass text with an emoji to the function

```
converting_emojis(text1)
```

```
#output
What are you saying face_with_tears_of_joy. I am the boss
smiling_face_with_sunglasses, and why are you so unamused_face
```

Problem

You want to remove emoji

Solution

The simplest way is to use Unicode.

How It Works

Follow these next steps.

Step 10-B1. Read the text data

```
#create sample text data with emoji
text1 = "What are you saying 😄. I am the boss😎, and why are you so 😒"
```

Step 10-B2. Install and import necessary libraries

```
#Importing libraries
import re
from emot.emo_unicode import UNICODE_EMO, EMOTICONS
```

Step 10-B3. Write a function to remove emojis

```
def emoji_removal(string):
    emoji_unicodes = re.compile("["
                                u"\U0001F600-\U0001F64F"  # emoticons
                                u"\U0001F300-\U0001F5FF"  # symbols
                                u"\U0001F680-\U0001F6FF"  # transport
```

```
            u"\U0001F1E0-\U0001F1FF"   # flags (iOS)
            u"\U00002500-\U00002BEF"
            u"\U00002702-\U000027B0"
            u"\U000024C2-\U0001F251"
            u"\U0001f926-\U0001f937"
            u"\U00010000-\U0010ffff"
            u"\u2640-\u2642"
            u"\u2600-\u2B55"
            u"\u200d"
            u"\u23cf"
            u"\u23e9"
            u"\u231a"
            u"\ufe0f"
            u"\u3030"
            "]+", flags=re.UNICODE)
    return emoji_unicodes.sub(r'', string)
```

Step 10-B4. Pass text with an emoji to the function

```
emoji_removal(text1)

#output
What are you saying. I am the boss, and why are you so emoji_removal
```

Problem

You want to replace emoticons with relevant, meaningful words.

Solution

The simplest way is to use the emot library.

How It Works

Follow these next steps.

Step 10-C1. Read the text data

```
#create sample text data with emoticons
text2 = "Hey, how are you :-) how was your day, what are you doing?:-)"
```

Step 10-C2. Install and import necessary libraries

```
#Installing emot library
!pip install emot
#Importing libraries
import re
from emot.emo_unicode import UNICODE_EMO, EMOTICONS
```

Step 10-C3. Write function to convert emoticons into word

```
# Function to convert emoticons into word
def converting_emoticons(text):
    for emot in EMOTICONS:
        text = re.sub(u'('+emot+')',
        "_".join(EMOTICONS[emot].replace(",","").split()), text)
    return text
```

Step 10-C4. Pass text with emoticons to the function

```
converting_emoticons(text2)
```

```
#output
Hey, how are you Happy_face_smiley how was your day, what are you doing?
Happy_face_smiley"
```

Problem

You want to remove emoticons

Solution

The simplest way is to use Unicode. The code for removing emojis and emoticons remains the same; however, you need to add the respective Unicode.

How It Works

Follow these next steps.

Step 10-D1 Read the text data

```
#create sample text data with emoticons
text2 = "Hey, how are you :-) how was your day, what are you doing?:-)"
```

Step 10-D2. Install and import necessary libraries

```
#Importing libraries
import re
from emot.emo_unicode import UNICODE_EMO, EMOTICONS
```

Step 10-D3. Write function to remove emoticons

```
def removing_emoticons(string):
    emot_unicodes = re.compile("["
                        u"\U0001F600-\U0001F64F"  # emoticons
                        u"\U0001F300-\U0001F5FF"  # symbols
                        u"\U0001F680-\U0001F6FF"  # transport
                        u"\U0001F1E0-\U0001F1FF"  # flags (iOS)
                        u"\U00002500-\U00002BEF"
                        u"\U00002702-\U000027B0"
                        u"\U000024C2-\U0001F251"
                        u"\U0001f926-\U0001f937"
                        u"\U00010000-\U0010ffff"
                        u"\u2640-\u2642"
                        u"\u2600-\u2B55"
                        u"\u200d"
                        u"\u23cf"
                        u"\u23e9"
                        u"\u231a"
                        u"\ufe0f"
                        u"\u3030"
                        "]+", flags=re.UNICODE)
    return emot_unicodes.sub(r'', string)
```

Step 10-D4. Pass text with emoticons to the function

```
removing_emoticons(text2)
```

```
#output
Hey, how are you how was your day, what are you doing?"
```

Problem

Find libraries that detect emojis and determine their meaning.

Solution

You can use the demoji library.

How It Works

Follow these next steps.

Step 10-E1. Read the text data

```
#create sample text data with emoji
text3 = """\
#Hey, I am going to say something special 🍼 that you are on 🔥 🐗
what is wrong with ⛏⛏ and it is so 👹 there are many... 🐵 🧧🎴 🧉⚖
again with the same issue ... 🔥🔥
MX and NI to find the best one of all 🔥🔥!!!!!.."""
```

Step 10-E2. Install and import necessary libraries

```
#Installing & Importing libraries
!pip install demoji
import demoji
demoji.download_codes()
```

Step 10-E3. Find all emojis and determine their meaning

```
demoji.findall(text3)
```

```
#Output:
```

```
{'🔥': 'fire',
 '🎅🏾': 'Santa Claus: medium-dark skin tone',
 '👨\u200d⚖️': 'man judge: medium skin tone',
 '🤡': 'clown face',
 '👹': 'ogre',
 '🌋': 'volcano',
 'NI': 'flag: Nicaragua',
 'MX': 'flag: Mexico',
 '🐂': 'ox',
 '🚣🏼': 'person rowing boat: medium-light skin tone'}
```

Recipe 2-11. Building a Text Preprocessing Pipeline

So far, you have completed most of the text manipulation and processing techniques and methods. Let's do something interesting in this recipe.

Problem

You want to build an end-to-end text preprocessing pipeline. Whenever you want to do preprocessing for any NLP application, you can directly plug data into this pipeline function and get the required clean text data as the output.

Solution

The simplest way is to create a custom function using all the techniques you have learned so far.

How It Works

It works by putting all the possible processing techniques into a wrapper function and passing the data through it.

Step 11-1. Read/create the text data

Let's create a list of strings and assign it to a variable—maybe a sample tweet.

```
tweet_sample= "How to take control of your #debt https://personal.vanguard.
com/us/insights/saving-investing/debt-management.#Best advice for #family
#financial #success (@PrepareToWin)"
```

You can also use your Twitter data extracted in Chapter 1.

Step 11-2. Process the text

Execute the following function to process the tweet.

```
def processRow(row):

    import re
    import nltk
    from textblob import TextBlob
    from nltk.corpus import stopwords
    from nltk.stem import PorterStemmer
    from textblob import Word
    from nltk.util import ngrams
    import re
    from wordcloud import WordCloud, STOPWORDS
    from nltk.tokenize import word_tokenize
    tweet = row
    #Lower case

    tweet.lower()
    #Removes unicode strings like "\u002c" and "x96"
    tweet = re.sub(r'(\\u[0-9A-Fa-f]+)', "r", tweet)
    tweet = re.sub(r'[^\x00-\x7f]', "r",tweet)
```

```
#convert any url to URL
tweet = re.sub('((www\.[^\s]+)|(https?://[^\s]+))','URL',tweet)
#Convert any @Username to "AT_USER"
tweet = re.sub('@[^\s]+','AT_USER',tweet)
#Remove additional white spaces
tweet = re.sub('[\s]+', ' ', tweet)
tweet = re.sub('[\n]+', ' ', tweet)
#Remove not alphanumeric symbols white spaces
tweet = re.sub(r'[^\w]', ' ', tweet)
#Removes hastag in front of a word """
tweet = re.sub(r'#([^\s]+)', r'\1', tweet)
#Replace #word with word
tweet = re.sub(r'#([^\s]+)', r'\1', tweet)
#Remove :( or :)
tweet = tweet.replace(':)',")
tweet = tweet.replace(':(',")
#remove numbers
tweet = ".join([i for i in tweet if not i.isdigit()])
#remove multiple exclamation
tweet = re.sub(r"(\!)\1+", ' ', tweet)
#remove multiple question marks
tweet = re.sub(r"(\?)\1+", ' ', tweet)
#remove multistop
tweet = re.sub(r"(\.)\1+", ' ', tweet)
#lemma
from textblob import Word
tweet =" ".join([Word(word).lemmatize() for word in tweet.split()])
#stemmer
#st = PorterStemmer()
#tweet=" ".join([st.stem(word) for word in tweet.split()])
#Removes emoticons from text
tweet = re.sub(':\)|;\)|:-\)|\(-:|:-D|=D|:P|xD|X-p|\^\^|:-*|
      \^\.\^|\^\-\^|\^\_\^|\,-\)|\)-:|:\'\(|:\(|:-\(|:\S|T\.T|
      \.\_\.|:<|:-\S|:-<|\*-\*|:0|=0|=\-0|0\.o|X0|0\_0|:-\@|=/|:/|
      X\-\(|>\.<|>=\(|D:', ", tweet)
```

```
    #trim
    tweet = tweet.strip('\'"')
    row = tweet

    return row
#call the function with your data
processRow(tweet_sample)
```

```
#output
'How to take control of your debt URL Best advice for family financial
success AT_USER'
```

So far, you have learned how to read text data and then process and clean it. The next chapter looks at converting text into meaningful features that build NLP applications.

CHAPTER 3

Converting Text to Features

This chapter covers basic to advanced feature engineering (text to features) methods. By the end of the chapter, you will be comfortable with the following recipes.

- Recipe 1. One-hot encoding

- Recipe 2. Count vectorizer

- Recipe 3. n-grams

- Recipe 4. Co-occurrence matrix

- Recipe 5. Hash vectorizing

- Recipe 6. Term frequency-inverse document frequency (TF-IDF)

- Recipe 7. Word embedding

- Recipe 8. Implementing fastText

- Recipe 9. Converting text to features using state-of-the-art embeddings

Now that all the text preprocessing steps have been discussed, let's explore feature engineering, the foundation for natural language processing. As you know, machines or algorithms cannot understand characters, words, or sentences. They can only take numbers as input, which includes binaries. But the inherent nature of textual data is unstructured and noisy, which makes it impossible to interact with machines.

The procedure of converting raw text into a machine-understandable format (numbers) is called feature engineering. The performance and accuracy of machine learning and deep learning algorithms are fundamentally dependent on the feature engineering technique.

This chapter discusses different feature engineering methods and techniques; their functionalities, advantages, and disadvantages; and examples to help you realize the importance of feature engineering.

© Akshay Kulkarni and Adarsha Shivananda 2021
A. Kulkarni and A. Shivananda, *Natural Language Processing Recipes*,
https://doi.org/10.1007/978-1-4842-7351-7_3

Recipe 3-1. Converting Text to Features Using One-Hot Encoding

One-hot encoding is the traditional method used in feature engineering. Anyone who knows the basics of machine learning has come across one-hot encoding. It is the process of converting categorical variables into features or columns and coding one or zero for that particular category. The same logic is used here, and the number of features is the number of total tokens present in the corpus.

Problem

You want to convert text to a feature using one-hot encoding.

Solution

One-hot encoding converts characters or words into binary numbers, as shown next.

	I	love	NLP	is	Future
I love NLP	1	1	1	0	0
NLP is future	0	0	1	1	1

How It Works

There are many functions to generate one-hot encoding features. Let's take one function and discuss it in depth.

Step 1-1. Store the text in a variable

The following shows a single line.

```
Text = "I am learning NLP"
```

Step 1-2. Execute a function on the text data

The following is a function from the pandas library to convert text into a feature.

```
# Importing the library

import pandas as pd

# Generating the features

pd.get_dummies(Text.split())
```

```
    Result :

    I  NLP  am  learning
0   1    0   0         0
1   0    0   1         0
2   0    0   0         1
3   0    1   0         0
```

The output has four features since the number of distinct words present in the input was 4.

Recipe 3-2. Converting Text to Features Using a Count Vectorizer

The approach used in Recipe 3-1 has a disadvantage. It does not consider the frequency of a word. If a particular word appears multiple times, there is a chance of missing information if it is not included in the analysis. A *count vectorizer* solves that problem. This recipe covers another method for converting text to a feature: the count vectorizer.

Problem

How do you convert text to a feature using a count vectorizer?

Solution

A count vectorizer is similar to one-hot encoding, but instead of checking whether a particular word is present or not, it counts the words that are present in the document.

In the following example, the words I and NLP occur twice in the first document.

	I	love	NLP	is	future	will	learn	In	2month
I love NLP and I will learn NLP in 2 months	2	1	2	0	0	1	1	1	1
NLP is future	0	0	1	1	1	0	0	0	0

How It Works

sklearn has a feature extraction function that extracts features out of text. Let's look at how to execute this. The following imports the CountVectorizer function from sklearn.

```
#importing the function

from sklearn.feature_extraction.text import CountVectorizer

# Text

text = ["I love NLP and I will learn NLP in 2month "]

# create the transform

vectorizer = CountVectorizer()

# tokenizing

vectorizer.fit(text)

# encode document

vector = vectorizer.transform(text)

# summarize & generating output

print(vectorizer.vocabulary_)
print(vector.toarray())
```

Result:

```
{'love': 4, 'nlp': 5, 'and': 1, 'will': 6, 'learn': 3, 'in': 2, '2month': 0}
[[1 1 1 1 1 2 1]]
```

The fifth token, nlp, appears twice in the document.

Recipe 3-3. Generating n-grams

In the preceding methods, each word was considered a feature. There is a drawback to this method. It does not consider the previous words and the next words to see if it would give a proper and complete meaning. For example, consider the phrase not bad. If it is split into individual words, it loses out on conveying good, which is what this phrase means.

As you saw, you could lose potential information or insights because many words make sense once they are put together. n-grams can solve this problem.

n-grams are the fusion of multiple letters or multiple words. They are formed in such a way that even the previous and next words are captured.

- Unigrams are the unique words present in a sentence.

- A bigram is the combination of two words.

- A trigram is the combination of three words. And so on.

For example, look at the sentence, "I am learning NLP."

- Unigrams: "I", "am", "learning", "NLP"

- Bigrams: "I am", "am learning", "learning NLP"

- Trigrams: "I am learning", "am learning NLP"

Problem

Generate the n-grams for a given sentence.

Solution

There are a lot of packages that generate n-grams. TextBlob is the most commonly used.

How It Works

Follow the steps in this section.

Step 3-1. Generate n-grams using TextBlob

Let's look at how to generate n-grams using TextBlob.

```
Text = "I am learning NLP"
```

Use the following TextBlob function to create n-grams. Use the text that is defined and state the n based on the requirement.

```
#Import textblob
from textblob import TextBlob

#For unigram : Use n = 1

TextBlob(Text).ngrams(1)
```

This is the output.

```
[WordList(['I']), WordList(['am']), WordList(['learning']),
WordList(['NLP'])]

#For Bigram : For bigrams, use n = 2

TextBlob(Text).ngrams(2)

[WordList(['I', 'am']),
 WordList(['am', 'learning']),
 WordList(['learning', 'NLP'])]
```

There are three lists with two words in an instance.

Step 3-2. Generate bigram-based features for a document

Just like in the last recipe, a count vectorizer to generates features. Using the same function, let's generate bigram features to see what the output looks like.

```
#importing the function

from sklearn.feature_extraction.text import CountVectorizer

# Text

text = ["I love NLP and I will learn NLP in 2month "]

# create the transform

vectorizer = CountVectorizer(ngram_range=(2,2))

# tokenizing

vectorizer.fit(text)

# encode document

vector = vectorizer.transform(text)

# summarize & generating output
print(vectorizer.vocabulary_)
print(vector.toarray())
```

This is the result.

```
{'love nlp': 3, 'nlp and': 4, 'and will': 0, 'will learn': 6, 'learn nlp': 2,
'nlp in': 5, 'in 2month': 1}
[[1 1 1 1 1 1 1]]
```

The output has features with bigrams; in the example, the count is 1 for all tokens. You can similarly use trigrams.

Recipe 3-4. Generating a Co-occurrence Matrix

Let's discuss a feature engineering method called a co-occurrence matrix.

Problem

You want to understand and generate a co-occurrence matrix.

Solution

A co-occurrence matrix is like a count vectorizer; it counts the occurrence of a group of words rather than individual words.

How It Works

Let's look at generating this kind of matrix using NLTK, bigrams, and some basic Python coding skills.

Step 4-1. Import the necessary libraries

Here is the code.

```
import numpy as np
import nltk
from nltk import bigrams
import itertools
```

Step 4-2. Create function for a co-occurrence matrix

The following is the co_occurrence_matrix function.

```
def co_occurrence_matrix(corpus):
    vocab = set(corpus)
    vocab = list(vocab)
    vocab_to_index = { word:i for i, word in enumerate(vocab) }
    # Create bigrams from all words in corpus
    bi_grams = list(bigrams(corpus))
    # Frequency distribution of bigrams ((word1, word2), num_occurrences)
    bigram_freq = nltk.FreqDist(bi_grams).most_common(len(bi_grams))
    # Initialise co-occurrence matrix
    # co_occurrence_matrix[current][previous]
    co_occurrence_matrix = np.zeros((len(vocab), len(vocab)))

    # Loop through the bigrams taking the current and previous word,
    # and the number of occurrences of the bigram.
    for bigram in bigram_freq:
        current = bigram[0][1]
```

```
        previous = bigram[0][0]
        count = bigram[1]
        pos_current = vocab_to_index[current]
        pos_previous = vocab_to_index[previous]
        co_occurrence_matrix[pos_current][pos_previous] = count
    co_occurrence_matrix = np.matrix(co_occurrence_matrix)
    # return the matrix and the index
    return co_occurrence_matrix,vocab_to_index
```

Step 4-3. Generate a co-occurrence matrix

Here are the sentences for testing.

```
sentences = [['I', 'love', 'nlp'],
             ['I', 'love','to' 'learn'],
             ['nlp', 'is', 'future'],
             ['nlp', 'is', 'cool']]
```

```
# create one list using many lists
```

```
merged = list(itertools.chain.from_iterable(sentences))
matrix = co_occurrence_matrix(merged)
```

```
# generate the matrix
```

```
CoMatrixFinal = pd.DataFrame(matrix[0], index=vocab_to_index,
columns=vocab_to_index)
print(CoMatrixFinal)
```

	I	is	love	future	tolearn	cool	nlp
I	0.0	0.0	0.0	0.0	0.0	0.0	1.0
is	0.0	0.0	0.0	0.0	0.0	0.0	2.0
love	2.0	0.0	0.0	0.0	0.0	0.0	0.0
future	0.0	1.0	0.0	0.0	0.0	0.0	0.0
tolearn	0.0	0.0	1.0	0.0	0.0	0.0	0.0
cool	0.0	1.0	0.0	0.0	0.0	0.0	0.0
nlp	0.0	0.0	1.0	1.0	1.0	0.0	0.0

I, love, and *is, nlp* appeared together twice, and a few other words appeared only once.

Recipe 3-5. Hash Vectorizing

A count vectorizer and a co-occurrence matrix both have one limitation: the vocabulary can become very large and cause memory/computation issues.

A *hash vectorizer* is one way to solve this problem.

Problem

You want to understand and generate a hash vectorizer.

Solution

A hash vectorizer is memory efficient, and instead of storing tokens as strings, the vectorizer applies the <u>hashing trick</u> to encode them as numerical indexes. The downside is that it's one way, and once vectorized, the features cannot be retrieved.

How It Works

Let's look at an example using `sklearn`.

Step 5-1. Import the necessary libraries and create a document

Here's the code.

```
from sklearn.feature_extraction.text import HashingVectorizer

# list of text documents
text = ["The quick brown fox jumped over the lazy dog."]
```

Step 5-2. Generate a hash vectorizer matrix

Let's create a hash vectorizer matrix (`HashingVectorizer`) with a vector size of 10.

```
# transform
vectorizer = HashingVectorizer(n_features=10)

# create the hashing vector
vector = vectorizer.transform(text)
```

```
# summarize the vector
print(vector.shape)
print(vector.toarray())

(1, 10)
[[ 0.          0.57735027  0.      0.      0.    0.    0.
  -0.57735027  -0.57735027  0.      ]]
```

It created a vector of size 10, and now it can be used for any supervised/ unsupervised tasks.

Recipe 3-6. Converting Text to Features Using TF-IDF

The above-mentioned text-to-feature methods have a few drawbacks, hence the introduction of TF-IDF. The following are some of the disadvantages.

- Let's say a particular word appears in all the corpus documents. It achieves higher importance in our previous methods, but that may not be relevant to your case.

- TF-IDF reflects on how important a word is to a document in a collection and hence normalizes words that frequently appear in all the documents.

Problem

You want to convert text to features using TF-IDF.

Solution

Term frequency (TF) is the ratio of the count of a particular word present in a sentence to the total count of words in the same sentence. TF captures the importance of the word irrespective of the length of the document. For example, a word with a frequency of 3 in a sentence with 10 words is different from when the word length of the sentence is 100 words. It should have more importance in the first scenario, which is what TF does. **TF**(t) = (Number of times term t appears in a document) / (Total number of terms in the document).

Inverse document frequency (IDF) is a log of the ratio of the total number of rows to the number of rows in a particular document in which a word is present. IDF = log(N/n), where N is the total number of rows, and n is the number of rows in which the word was present.

IDF measures the rareness of a term. Words like *a* and *the* show up in all the corpus documents, but rare words are not in all documents. So, if a word appears in almost all the documents, that word is of no use since it does not help with classification or information retrieval. IDF nullifies this problem.

TF-IDF is the simple product of TF and IDF that addresses both drawbacks, making predictions and information retrieval relevant.

$$TF\text{-}IDF = TF * IDF$$

How It Works

Follow the steps in this section.

Step 6-1. Read the text data

The following is a familiar phrase.

```
Text = ["The quick brown fox jumped over the lazy dog.",
"The dog.",
"The fox"]
```

Step 6-2. Create the features

Execute the following code on the text data.

```
#Import TfidfVectorizer

from sklearn.feature_extraction.text import TfidfVectorizer

#Create the transform

vectorizer = TfidfVectorizer()

#Tokenize and build vocab

vectorizer.fit(Text)
```

```
#Summarize

print(vectorizer.vocabulary_)
print(vectorizer.idf_)
```

This is the result.

```
Text = ["The quick brown fox jumped over the lazy dog.",
"The dog.",
"The fox"]

{'the': 7, 'quick': 6, 'brown': 0, 'fox': 2, 'jumped': 3, 'over': 5,
 'lazy': 4, 'dog': 1}
[ 1.69314718  1.28768207  1.28768207  1.69314718   1.69314718
   1.69314718  1.69314718  1.    ]
```

Observe that the appears in all three documents, so it does not add much value. The vector value is 1, which is less than all the other tokens.

All the methods or techniques you have looked at so far are based on frequency. They are called frequency-based embeddings or features. The next recipe looks at prediction-based embeddings, typically called word embeddings.

Recipe 3-7. Implementing Word Embeddings

This recipe assumes that you have a working knowledge of how a neural network works and the mechanisms by which weights in the neural network are updated. If you are new to neural networks, we suggest that you go through Chapter 6 to gain a basic understanding of how a neural network works.

Even though all the previous methods solve most problems, once you get into more complex problems where you want to capture the semantic relation between words (context), these methods fail to perform.

The following explains the challenges with the methods discussed so far.

- The techniques fail to capture the context and meaning of the words. They depend on the appearance or frequency of words. You need to know how to capture the context or semantic relationships.

  a. I am eating an *apple*.

  b. I am using an *Apple*.

In the example, *apple* has different meanings when it is used with different (close by) adjacent words *eating* and *using*.

- For a problem like a document classification (book classification in the library), a document is huge, and many tokens are generated. In these scenarios, your number of features can get out of control (wherein), thus hampering the accuracy and performance.

A machine/algorithm can match two documents/texts and say whether they are the same or not. How do we make machines talk about cricket or Virat Kohli when you search for MS Dhoni? How do you make the machine understand that the word *apple* in "An apple is a tasty fruit" is a fruit that can be eaten and not a company?

The answer to these questions lies in creating a representation for words that capture their meanings, semantic relationships, and the different types of contexts they are used in.

Word embeddings address these challenges. A word embedding is a feature-learning technique in which vocabulary are mapped to vectors of real numbers, capturing contextual hierarchy.

In the following table, every word is represented by four numbers, called vectors. Using the word embeddings technique, we derived those vectors for each word to use them in future analysis and building applications. In the example, the dimension is four, but you usually use a dimension greater than 100.

Words	Vectors			
text	0.36	0.36	-0.43	0.36
idea	-0.56	-0.56	0.72	-0.56
word	0.35	-0.43	0.12	0.72
encode	0.19	0.19	0.19	0.43
document	-0.43	0.19	-0.43	0.43
grams	0.72	-0.43	0.72	0.12
process	0.43	0.72	0.43	0.43
feature	0.12	0.45	0.12	0.87

Problem

You want to implement word embeddings.

Solution

Word embeddings are prediction-based, and they use shallow neural networks to train the model that leads to learning the weight and using them as a vector representation.

word2vec is the deep learning Google framework to train word embeddings. It uses all the words of the whole corpus and predicts the nearby words. It creates a vector for all the words present in the corpus so that the context is captured. It also outperforms any other methodologies in the space of word similarity and word analogies.

There are mainly two types in word2vec.

- skip-gram

- Continuous Bag of Words (CBOW)

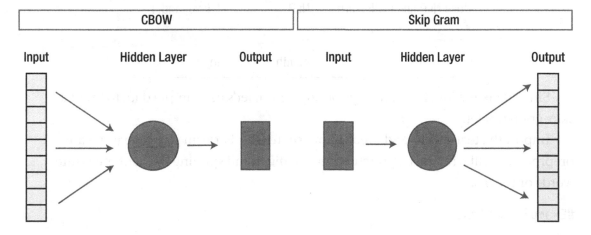

How It Works

The above figure shows the architecture of the CBOW and skip-gram algorithms used to build word embeddings. Let's look at how these models work.

skip-gram

The skip-gram model[1] predicts the probabilities of a word given the context of the word or words.

---

[1] https://arxiv.org/abs/1310.4546

Let's take a small sentence and understand how it works. Each sentence generates a target word and context, which are the words nearby. The number of words to be considered around the target variable is called the window size. The following table shows all the possible target and context variables for window size 2. Window size needs to be selected based on data and the resources at your disposal. The larger the window size, the higher the computing power.

Text = "I love NLP and I will learn NLP in 2 months"

	Target word	Context
I love NLP	I	love, NLP
I love NLP and	love	love, NLP, and
I love NLP and I will learn	NLP	I, love, and, I
…	…	…
in 2 months	month	in, 2

Since it takes a lot of text and computing power, let's use sample data to build a skip-gram model.

Import the text corpus and break it into sentences. Perform some cleaning and preprocessing like removing punctuation and digits and splitting the sentences into words or tokens.

```
#Example sentences

sentences = [['I', 'love', 'nlp'],
             ['I', 'will', 'learn', 'nlp', 'in', '2','months'],
             ['nlp', 'is', 'future'],
             ['nlp', 'saves', 'time', 'and', 'solves', 'lot', 'of',
              'industry', 'problems'],
             ['nlp', 'uses', 'machine', 'learning']]

#import library

!pip install gensim

import gensim
from gensim.models import Word2Vec
from sklearn.decomposition import PCA
from matplotlib import pyplot
```

```
# training the model

skipgram = Word2Vec(sentences, size =50, window = 3, min_count=1,sg = 1)
print(skipgram)

# access vector for one word

print(skipgram['nlp'])

[ 0.00552227 -0.00723104  0.00857073  0.00368054 -0.00071274  0.00837146
   0.00179965 -0.0049786  -0.00448666 -0.00182289  0.00857488 -0.00499459
   0.00188365 -0.0093498   0.00174774 -0.00609793 -0.00533857 -0.007905
  -0.00176814 -0.00024082 -0.00181886 -0.00093836 -0.00382601 -0.00986026
   0.00312014 -0.00821249  0.00787507 -0.00864689 -0.00686584 -0.00370761
   0.0056183   0.00859488 -0.00163146  0.00928791  0.00904601  0.00443816
  -0.00192308  0.00941    -0.00202355 -0.00756564 -0.00105471  0.00170084
   0.00606918 -0.00848301 -0.00543473  0.00747958  0.0003408   0.00512787
  -0.00909613  0.00683905]
```

Since our vector size parameter was 50, the model gives a vector of size 50 for each word.

```
# access vector for another one word

print(skipgram['deep'])

KeyError: "word 'deep' not in vocabulary"
```

We get an error saying the word doesn't exist because this word was not in our input training data. We need to train the algorithm on as large a dataset as possible so that we do not miss words.

There is one more way to tackle this problem. Read Recipe 3-6 for the answer.

```
# save model

skipgram.save('skipgram.bin')

# load model

skipgram = Word2Vec.load('skipgram.bin')
```

A t-SNE plot is one of the ways to evaluate word embeddings. Let's generate it and see how it looks.

```
# T - SNE plot

X = skipgram[skipgram.wv.vocab]
pca = PCA(n_components=2)
result = pca.fit_transform(X)

# create a scatter plot of the projection

pyplot.scatter(result[:, 0], result[:, 1])
words = list(skipgram.wv.vocab)
for i, word in enumerate(words):
        pyplot.annotate(word, xy=(result[i, 0], result[i, 1]))
pyplot.show()
```

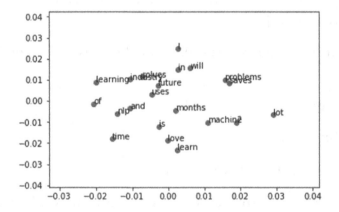

Continuous Bag of Words (CBOW)

Now let's look at how to build a CBOW model.

```
#import library

from gensim.models import Word2Vec
from sklearn.decomposition import PCA
from matplotlib import pyplot
```

```
#Example sentences

sentences = [['I', 'love', 'nlp'],
                ['I', 'will', 'learn', 'nlp', 'in', '2','months'],
                ['nlp', 'is', 'future'],
                ['nlp', 'saves', 'time', 'and', 'solves', 'lot', 'of',
                 'industry', 'problems'],
                ['nlp', 'uses', 'machine', 'learning']]

# training the model

cbow = Word2Vec(sentences, size =50, window = 3, min_count=1,sg = 1)
print(cbow)

# access vector for one word

print(cbow['nlp'])

# save model

cbow.save('cbow.bin')

# load model

cbow = Word2Vec.load('cbow.bin')

# T - SNE plot

X = cbow[cbow.wv.vocab]
pca = PCA(n_components=2)
result = pca.fit_transform(X)

# create a scatter plot of the projection

pyplot.scatter(result[:, 0], result[:, 1])
words = list(cbow.wv.vocab)
for i, word in enumerate(words):
        pyplot.annotate(word, xy=(result[i, 0], result[i, 1]))
pyplot.show()
```

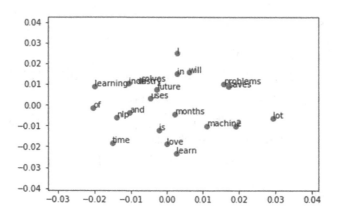

Training these models requires a huge amount of computing power. Let's use Google's pre-trained model, which has been trained with more than 100 billion words.

Download the model from `https://drive.google.com/file/d/0B7XkCwpI5KDYNlNUTTlSS21pQmM/edit` and keep it in your local storage.

`https://drive.google.com/file/d/0B7XkCwpI5KDYNlNUTTlSS21pQmM/edit`

Import the gensim package and follow the steps to learn Google's word2vec.

```
# import gensim package

import gensim

# load the saved model

model = gensim.models.Word2Vec.load_word2vec_format
        ('C:\\Users\\GoogleNews-vectors-negative300.bin', binary=True)

#Checking how similarity works.

print (model.similarity('this', 'is'))

Output:
0.407970363878

#Lets check one more.
print (model.similarity('post', 'book'))

Output:
0.0572043891977
```

This and is have a good amount of similarity, but the similarity between the words post and book is poor. For any given set of words, it uses the vectors of both the words and calculates the similarity between them.

```
# Finding the odd one out.
```

```
model.doesnt_match('breakfast cereal dinner lunch';.split())
```

The output is

```
'cereal'
```

Among *breakfast, cereal, dinner,* and *lunch,* the word cereal is the least related to all the other three words.

```
# It is also finding the relations between words.
```

```
word_vectors.most_similar(positive=['woman', 'king'], negative=['man'])
```

This is the output.

```
queen: 0.7699
```

If you add *woman* and *king* and subtract man, it predicts queen as the output with 77% confidence. Isn't this amazing?

king ✚ woman ▬ man ⟶ queen

Let's look at a few interesting examples using the t-SNE plot for word embeddings, such as for home interiors and exteriors. For example, all the words related to electrical fittings are near each other; similarly, words related to bathroom fittings are near each other, and so on. This is the beauty of word embeddings.

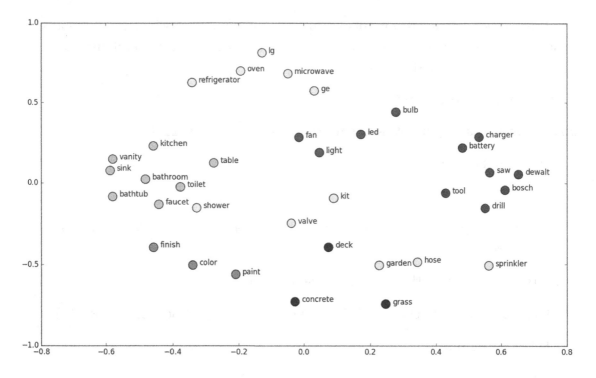

Recipe 3-8. Implementing fastText

fastText is another deep learning framework developed by Facebook to capture context and generate a feature vector.

Problem

You want to learn how to implement fastText in Python.

Solution

fastText is the improvised version of word2vec, which considers words to build the representation. But fastText takes each character while computing a word's representation.

How It Works

Let's look at how to build a fastText word embedding.

```python
# Import FastText

from gensim.models import FastText
from sklearn.decomposition import PCA
from matplotlib import pyplot

#Example sentences

sentences = [['I', 'love', 'nlp'],
             ['I', 'will', 'learn', 'nlp', 'in', '2','months'],
             ['nlp', 'is', 'future'],
             ['nlp', 'saves', 'time', 'and', 'solves', 'lot', 'of',
              'industry', 'problems'],
             ['nlp', 'uses', 'machine', 'learning']]

fast = FastText(sentences,size=20, window=1, min_count=1, workers=5,
min_n=1, max_n=2)

# vector for word nlp

print(fast['nlp'])
```

```
[-0.00459182  0.00607472 -0.01119007  0.00555629 -0.00781679  -0.01376211
   0.00675235 -0.00840158 -0.00319737  0.00924599  0.00214165  -0.01063819
   0.01226836  0.00852781  0.01361119 -0.00257012  0.00819397  -0.00410289
  -0.0053979  -0.01360016]
```

```python
# vector for word deep

print(fast['deep'])
```

```
[ 0.00271002 -0.00242539 -0.00771885 -0.00396854  0.0114902   -0.00640606
   0.00637542 -0.01248098 -0.01207364  0.01400793 -0.00476079  -0.00230879
   0.02009759 -0.01952532  0.01558956 -0.01581665  0.00510567  -0.00957186
  -0.00963234 -0.02059373]
```

This is the advantage of using fastText. The word deep was not present in training word2vec, and we did not get a vector for that word. But since fastText is building the character level, it provides results—even for a word that was not there in training. You can see the vector for the word deep.

```
# load model

fast = Word2Vec.load('fast.bin')

# visualize

X = fast[fast.wv.vocab]
pca = PCA(n_components=2)
result = pca.fit_transform(X)

# create a scatter plot of the projection

pyplot.scatter(result[:, 0], result[:, 1])
words = list(fast.wv.vocab)
for i, word in enumerate(words):
        pyplot.annotate(word, xy=(result[i, 0], result[i, 1]))
pyplot.show()
```

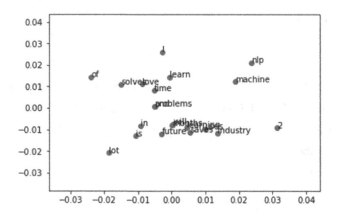

The figure above shows the embedding representation for fastText. If you observe closely, the words love and solve are close together in fastText but in your skip-gram and CBOW, love and learn are near to each other. This is because of character-level embeddings.

Recipe 3-9. Converting Text to Features Using State-of-the-Art Embeddings

Let's discuss and implement some advanced context-based feature engineering methods.

Problem

You want to learn text to features using state-of-the-art embeddings.

Solution

Let's discuss the following seven methods.

- GloVe Embedding

- ELMo

- Sentence encoders

  - doc2vec

  - Sentence-BERT

  - Universal Encoder

  - InferSent

- Open-AI GPT

GloVe is an alternate word embedding method to create vector subspace of the word. GloVe model trains on co-occurrence counts of words, and by minimizing least square error, it produces vector space.

In GloVe, you first construct co-occurrence: each row is a word, and each column is the context. This matrix calculates the frequency of words with context. Since the context dimension is very large, you want to reduce the context and learn a low-dimensional representation of word embedding. This process can be regarded as the reconstruction problem of the co-occurrence matrix, namely reconstruction loss. The motivation of GloVe is to explicitly force the model to learn such a relationship based on the co-occurrence matrix.

word2vec, skip-gram, and CBOW are predictive and ignore the fact that some context words occur more often than others. They only take into consideration the local context and hence failing to capture the global context.

While word2vec predicts the context of a given word, GloVe learns by constructing a co-occurrence matrix.

word2vec does not have global information embedded, while GloVe creates a global co-occurrence matrix counting frequency of context with each word. The presence of global information makes GloVe better.

GloVe does not learn by a neural network like word2vec. Instead, it has the simple loss function of the difference between the product of word embeddings and log of the probability of co-occurrence.

The research paper is at `https://nlp.stanford.edu/pubs/glove.pdf`.

ELMo

ELMo vectors are the vectors that are the function of a given sentence. The main advantage of this method is it can have different vectors of words under different contexts.

ELMo is a deep contextualized word representation model. It looks at complex characteristics of words (e.g., syntax and semantics), and studies how they vary across linguistic contexts (i.e., to model polysemy).

Word vectors are learned functions of the internal states of a deep bidirectional language model (biLM), which is pre-trained on a large text corpus.

Words with different contexts in different sentences are called polysemous words. ELMo can successfully handle words of this nature, which GloVe and fastText fail to capture.

The research paper is at `www.aclweb.org/anthology/N18-1202.pdf`.

Link to research paper: `https://www.aclweb.org/anthology/N18-1202.pdf`

Sentence Encoders

Why learned sentence embeddings? Traditional techniques use an average of the word embeddings to form sentence embeddings. But there are cons to this approach, such as the order of the words are not considered, and the similarities obtained by averaging word vectors are the same if the words are swapped in a sentence.

doc2vec

doc2vec is based on word2vec. Words maintain a grammatical structure, but documents don't have any grammatical structures. To solve this problem, another vector (paragraph ID) is added to the word2vec model. This is the only difference between word2vec and doc2vec.

word2vec calculates the mean of all vectors represented by words, while doc2vec directly represents a sentence as a vector. Like word2vec, there are two doc2vec models available.

- Distributed Memory Model of Paragraph Vectors (PV-DM)

- Distributed Bag of Words version of Paragraph Vector (PV-DBOW)

The distributed memory (DM) model is similar to the CBOW model. CBOW predicts the target word given its context as an input, whereas in doc2vec, a paragraph ID is added.

The Distributed Bag-Of-Words (DBOW) model is similar to the skip-gram model in word2vec, which predicts the context words from a target word. This model only takes paragraph ID as input and predicts context from the vocabulary.

The research paper is at https://cs.stanford.edu/~quocle/paragraph_vector.pdf.

Sentence-BERT

Sentence-BERT (SBERT) is a modification of the pre-trained BERT network that uses siamese and triplet network structures to derive semantically meaningful sentence embeddings that can be compared using cosine-similarity. This reduces the effort of finding the most similar pair from 65 hours with BERT/RoBERTa to about 5 seconds with SBERT while maintaining the accuracy from BERT.

The leader among the pack, Sentence-BERT, was introduced in 2018 and immediately took the pole position for sentence embeddings. There are four key concepts at the heart of this BERT-based model.

- Attention

- Transformers

- BERT

- Siamese networks

Sentences are passed to BERT models and a pooling layer to generate their embeddings.

The research paper is at www.aclweb.org/anthology/D19-1410.pdf.

Universal Encoder

The Universal Sentence Encoder model specifically targets transfer learning to the NLP tasks and generates embeddings.

It is trained on a variety of data sources to learn for a wide variety of tasks. The sources are Wikipedia, web news, web question-answer pages, and discussion forums. The input is variable-length English text, and the output is a 512-dimensional vector.

Sentence embeddings are calculated by averaging all the embeddings of the words in the sentence; however, just adding or averaging had limitations and was not suited for deriving the true semantic meaning of the sentence. The Universal Sentence Encoder makes getting sentence-level embeddings easy.

Two variants of the TensorFlow model allow for trade-offs between accuracy and computing resources.

- Transformers

- Deep Average Network

The research paper is at https://arxiv.org/pdf/1803.11175v2.pdf.

InferSent

In 2017, Facebook introduced InferSent as a sentence representation model trained using the Stanford Natural Language Inference datasets (SNLI). SNLI is a dataset of 570,000 English sentences, and each sentence is a pair sentence of the premise, hypothesis labeled in one of the following categories: entailment, contradiction, or neutral.

The research paper is at `https://arxiv.org/pdf/1705.02364.pdf`.

Open-AI GPT

The GPT (Generative Pre-trained Transformer) architecture implements a deep neural network, specifically a transformer model, which uses attention in place of previous recurrence-based and convolution-based architectures. Attention mechanisms allow the model to selectively focus on segments of input text it predicts to be the most relevant.

Due to the broadness of the dataset on which it is trained and the broadness of its approach, GPT became capable of performing a diverse range of tasks beyond simple text generation: answering questions, summarizing, and even translating between languages in a variety of specific domains.

The research paper is at `https://cdn.openai.com/better-language-models/language_models_are_unsupervised_multitask_learners.pdf`.

How It Works

Download the dataset from `www.kaggle.com/rounakbanik/ted-talks` and keep it in your local folder. Then follow the steps in this section.

Dataset link: `https://www.kaggle.com/rounakbanik/ted-talks`

Step 9-1. Import a notebook and data to Google Colab

Google Colab is used to solve this project given BERT models are huge, and building it in Colab is way easier and faster.

Go to Google Colab at `https://colab.research.google.com/notebooks/intro.ipynb`. `https://colab.research.google.com/notebooks/intro.ipynb`

Go to file and open a new notebook or Upload notebook from your local by selecting "Upload notebook".

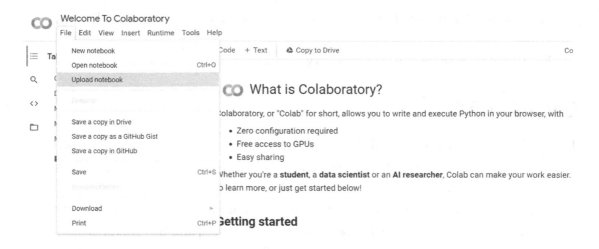

To import the data, go to Files, click the Upload to Session Storage option, and then import the csv file.

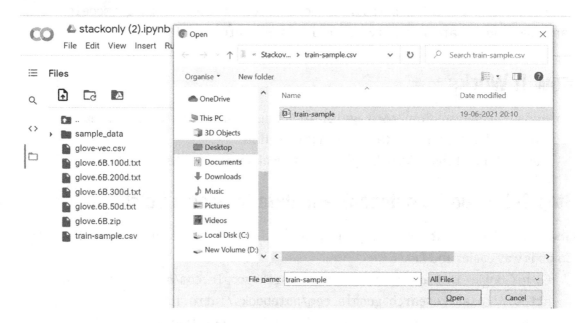

Step 9-2. Install and import libraries

```
#If any of these libraries are not installed, please install them using pip
before importing.

import pandas as pd
import numpy as np
import scipy
import os

import nltk
nltk.download('stopwords')
nltk.download('punkt')
ltk.download('wordnet')
import string
import csv
from nltk.tokenize import word_tokenize
from nltk.corpus import stopwords
from nltk.stem import WordNetLemmatizer # used for preprocessing
import warnings
warnings.filterwarnings('ignore')

from sklearn import preprocessing
import spacy
from tqdm import tqdm
import re
import matplotlib.pyplot as plt # our main display package
import plotly.graph_objects as go

import tensorflow_hub as hub
import tensorflow as tf
print(tf.__version__)
```

Step 9-3. Read text data

```
df = pd.read_csv('Ted talks.csv')

df_sample=df.iloc[0:100,:]
```

Step 9-4. Process text data

Let's implement the preprocessing steps that you learned in Chapter 2.

```python
# remove urls, handles, and the hashtag from hashtags
def remove_urls(text):
    new_text = ' '.join(re.sub("(@[A-Za-z0-9]+)|([^0-9A-Za-z \t])|
    (\w+:\/\/\S+)"," ",text).split())
    return new_text
# make all text lowercase
def text_lowercase(text):
    return text.lower()
# remove numbers
def remove_numbers(text):
    result = re.sub(r'\d+', '', text)
    return result
# remove punctuation
def remove_punctuation(text):
    translator = str.maketrans('', '', string.punctuation)
    return text.translate(translator)
# tokenize
def tokenize(text):
    text = word_tokenize(text)
    return text
# remove stopwords
stop_words = set(stopwords.words('english'))
def remove_stopwords(text):
    text = [i for i in text if not i in stop_words]
    return text
# lemmatize
lemmatizer = WordNetLemmatizer()
def lemmatize(text):
    text = [lemmatizer.lemmatize(token) for token in text]
    return text
```

```
def preprocessing(text):

    text = text_lowercase(text)
    text = remove_urls(text)
    text = remove_numbers(text)
    text = remove_punctuation(text)
    text = tokenize(text)
    text = remove_stopwords(text)
    text = lemmatize(text)
    text = ' '.join(text)
    return text

#preprocessing input
for i in range(df_sample.shape[0]):
    df_sample['description'][i]=preprocessing(str(df_sample['description']
    [i]))
#in case if description has next line character
for text in df_sample.description:
    text=text.replace('\n',' ')
```

Step 9-5. Generate a feature vector

```
#Implementations of above methods
#GloVe:
#loading pre-trained glove model
#downloading and unzipping all word embeddings
!wget http://nlp.stanford.edu/data/glove.6B.zip
!unzip glove*.zip
!ls
!pwd

#importing 100-d glove model
glove_model_100vec = pd.read_table("glove.6B.100d.txt", sep=" ",
index_col=0, header=None, quoting=csv.QUOTE_NONE)

# getting mean vector for each sentence
```

```python
def get_mean_vector(glove_model, words):
    # remove out-of-vocabulary words
    #assuming 100-d vector
    words = [word for word in word_tokenize(words) if word in
    list(glove_model_100vec.index)] #if word is in vocab
    if len(words) >= 1:
        return np.mean(glove_model_100vec.loc[words].values, axis=0)
    else:
        return np.array([0]*100)

#creating empty list and appending all mean arrays for comparing cosine
similarities
glove_vec=[]
for i in df_sample.description:
    glove_vec.append(list(get_mean_vector(glove_model_100vec, i)))

glove_vec=np.asarray(glove_vec)
glove_vec

    #output

array([[-0.11690753,  0.17445151,  0.04606778, ..., -0.48718723,
         0.28744267,  0.16625453],
       [-0.12658561,  0.17125735,  0.44709804, ..., -0.18936391,
         0.51547109,  0.2958283 ],
       [-0.06018609,  0.12372995,  0.27105957, ..., -0.38565426,
         0.39135596,  0.2519755 ],
       ...,
       [-0.12469988,  0.11091088,  0.16328073, ..., -0.08730062,
         0.25822592,  0.12540627],
       [ 0.09014104,  0.09796044,  0.13403036, ..., -0.371885  ,
         0.19138244,  0.05781978],
       [ 0.00891036,  0.09064478,  0.22670132, ..., -0.26099886,
         0.47415786,  0.30951336]])
```

ELMo:

```
# Due to some open issue with TensorFlow Hub on latest version (2.x), we
are degrading to tensorflow 1.x version
#!pip uninstall tensorflow
!pip install tensorflow==1.15

import tensorflow as tf
import tensorflow_hub as hub
print(tf.__version__)

#Load pre-trained model
embed_ = hub.Module("https://tfhub.dev/google/elmo/3")

#function to average word vectors of each sentence
def elmo_vectors_sentence(x):
  sentence_embeddings = embed_(x.tolist(), signature="default",
  as_dict=True)["elmo"]

  with tf.Session() as sess:
    sess.run(tf.global_variables_initializer())
    sess.run(tf.tables_initializer())
    # Average of each vector
    return sess.run(tf.reduce_mean(sentence_embeddings,1))

#if your data set is large , make a batch of 100 samples. Just remove comment
and run the code given below. As we have just 100 samples, we are not doing this
 #samples= [df[i:i+100] for i in range(0,df.shape[0],100)]
 # elmo_vec = [elmo_vectors_sentence(x['description']) for x in samples]
 #elmo_vec_full= np.concatenate(elmo_vec, axis = 0)

#embeddings on our dataset
elmo_vec = elmo_vectors_sentence(df_sample['description'])

elmo_vec
```

#output

```
array([[ 0.0109894 , -0.16668989, -0.06553215, ...,  0.07014981,
         0.09196191,  0.04669906],
       [ 0.15317157, -0.19256656,  0.01390844, ...,  0.03459582,
         0.28029835,  0.11106762],
       [ 0.20210212, -0.13186318, -0.20647219, ..., -0.15281932,
         0.12729007,  0.17192583],
       ...,
       [ 0.29017407, -0.45098212,  0.0250571 , ..., -0.12281103,
         0.23303834,  0.15486737],
       [ 0.22871418,  0.12254314, -0.22637479, ...,  0.04150296,
         0.31900924,  0.28121516],
       [ 0.05940952,  0.01366339, -0.17502695, ...,  0.20946877,
         0.0020928 ,  0.1114894 ]], dtype=float32)
```

Doc2Vec:

```
#importing doc2vec and tagged document
from gensim.models.doc2vec import Doc2Vec, TaggedDocument

#tokenizing data
tokenized_data=[word_tokenize(word) for word in df_sample.description]

train_data=[TaggedDocument(d, [i]) for i, d in enumerate(tokenized_
data)]    #adding paragraph id as mentioned in explanation for training
train_data
```

#output

```
[TaggedDocument(words=['sir', 'ken', 'robinson', 'make', 'entertaining',
'profoundly', 'moving', 'case', 'creating', 'education', 'system',
'nurture', 'rather', 'undermines', 'creativity'], tags=[0]),
 TaggedDocument(words=['humor', 'humanity', 'exuded', 'inconvenient',
'truth', 'al', 'gore', 'spell', 'way', 'individual', 'address', 'climate',
'change', 'immediately', 'buying', 'hybrid', 'inventing', 'new', 'hotter',
'brand', 'name', 'global', 'warming'], tags=[1]),
```

```
TaggedDocument(words=['new', 'york', 'time', 'columnist', 'david',
'pogue', 'take', 'aim', 'technology', 'worst', 'interface', 'design',
'offender', 'provides', 'encouraging', 'example', 'product', 'get',
'right', 'funny', 'thing', 'burst', 'song'], tags=[2]),
TaggedDocument(words=['emotionally', 'charged', 'talk', 'macarthur',
'winning', 'activist', 'majora', 'carter', 'detail', 'fight',
'environmental', 'justice', 'south', 'bronx', 'show', 'minority',
'neighborhood', 'suffer', 'flawed', 'urban', 'policy'], tags=[3]),
TaggedDocument(words=['never', 'seen', 'data', 'presented', 'like',
'drama', 'urgency', 'sportscaster', 'statistic', 'guru', 'han', 'rosling',
'debunks', 'myth', 'called', 'developing', 'world'], tags=[4])

    ..........

## Train doc2vec model
model = Doc2Vec(train_data, vector_size = 100, window = 2, min_count = 1,
epochs = 100)

def get_vectors(model,words):
  words = [word for word in word_tokenize(words) if word in
          list(model.wv.vocab)]
  #words = [word for word in word_tokenize(words) if word in
          list(model.wv.index_to_key)] #if gensim version is >4.0.0 ,use
          this line
  if len(words)>=1:
    return model.infer_vector(words)
  else:
    return np.array([0]*100)

#defining empty list
doc2vec_vec=[]
for i in df_sample.description:
    doc2vec_vec.append(list(get_vectors(model, i)))

doc2vec_vec=np.asarray(doc2vec_vec)

doc2vec_vec
```

```
#output
array([[ 0.00505156, -0.582084  , -0.33430266, ...,  0.29665616,
        -0.5472022 ,  0.48537165],
       [ 0.05787622, -0.6559785 , -0.41140306, ...,  0.24132295,
        -0.73182726,  0.6089837 ],
       [ 0.02416484, -0.48238695, -0.29850838, ...,  0.2710957 ,
        -0.51971895,  0.4405582 ],
       ...,
       [ 0.0511999 , -0.5991625 , -0.34839907, ...,  0.29519215,
        -0.68761116,  0.4545323 ],
       [ 0.0180944 , -0.8318272 , -0.3488748 , ...,  0.30490136,
        -0.7558393 ,  0.56117946],
       [-0.04790357, -0.66188   , -0.3797214 , ...,  0.34476635,
        -0.7202311 ,  0.5834031 ]], dtype=float32)
```

Sentence-BERT

```
#BERT sentence transformer for sentence encoding
!pip install sentence-transformers

#importing bert-base model

from sentence_transformers import SentenceTransformer
sbert_model = SentenceTransformer('bert-base-nli-mean-tokens')

#one more model to try
#model = SentenceTransformer('paraphrase-MiniLM-L12-v2')

#embeding on description column
sentence_embeddings_BERT = sbert_model.encode(df_sample['description'])
print('Sample BERT embedding vector - length',
len(sentence_embeddings_BERT[0]))
```

#output

Sample BERT embedding vector - length 768

sentence_embeddings_BERT
```
array([[-0.31804532,  0.6571422 ,  0.5327481 , ..., -0.76469   ,
         -0.4919126 ,  0.1543465 ],
       [-0.08962823,  1.0855986 ,  0.37181526, ..., -0.84685326,
         0.5427714 ,  0.32389015],
       [-0.13385592,  0.8280815 ,  0.76139224, ..., -0.33403403,
         0.2664094 , -0.05493931],
       ...,
       [ 0.05133615,  1.1150284 ,  0.75921553, ...,  0.5516633 ,
         0.46614835,  0.28827885],
       [-1.3568689 ,  0.2995725 ,  0.99510914, ...,  0.26881158,
         -0.1879525 ,  0.18646894],
       [-0.20679009,  0.8725009 ,  1.2933054 , ..., -0.44921246,
         0.14516312, -0.2050481 ]], dtype=float32)
```

sentence_embeddings_BERT.shape

#output

(100, 768)

Universal Encoder

#Load the pre-trained model

```
module_url = "https://tfhub.dev/google/universal-sentence-encoder/4"
model_USE = hub.load(module_url)

embeddings_USE = model_USE(df_sample['description'])

embeddings_USE = tf.reshape(embeddings_USE,[100,512])

embeddings_USE.shape
```

```
    #output
```

```
TensorShape([Dimension(100), Dimension(512)])
```

```
#output is tensor
```

Infersent

There are two versions of InferSent. Version 1 uses GloVe, whereas version 2 uses fastText vectors. You can choose to work with any model. We used version 2, so we downloaded the InferSent model and the pre-trained word vectors.

```
! mkdir encoder
! curl -Lo encoder/infersent2.pkl https://dl.fbaipublicfiles.com/infersent/
  infersent2.pkl
```

```
! mkdir GloVe
! curl -Lo GloVe/glove.840B.300d.zip http://nlp.stanford.edu/data/
  glove.840B.300d.zip
! unzip GloVe/glove.840B.300d.zip -d GloVe/
```

```
! unzip GloVe/glove.840B.300d.zip -d GloVe/
```

```
from models import InferSent
import torch
```

```
V = 2
MODEL_PATH = '/content/drive/MyDrive/yolov3/encoder/infersent%s.pkl' % V
params_model = {'bsize': 64, 'word_emb_dim': 300, 'enc_lstm_dim': 2048,
                'pool_type': 'max', 'dpout_model': 0.0, 'version': V}
model_infer = InferSent(params_model)
model_infer.load_state_dict(torch.load(MODEL_PATH))
```

```
W2V_PATH = '/content/drive/MyDrive/yolov3/GloVe/glove.840B.300d.txt'
model_infer.set_w2v_path(W2V_PATH)
```

```
#building vocabulary
model_infer.build_vocab(df_sample.description, tokenize=True)
```

```
    #output
```

```
Found 1266(/1294) words with w2v vectors
Vocab size : 1266
```

```
#encoding sample dataset
```

```
infersent_embed = model_infer.encode(df_sample.description,tokenize=True)
```

```
#shape of our vector
infersent_embed.shape
```

```
    #output
```

```
(100, 4096)
```

```
get_embed(df_sample,'infersent')
```

```
    #output
```

```
array([[ 0.00320979,  0.0560745 ,  0.11894835, ...,  0.04763867,
         0.02359796,  0.09751415],
       [ 0.00983471,  0.11757359,  0.12201475, ...,  0.06545023,
         0.04181211,  0.07941461],
       [-0.02874381,  0.18418473,  0.12211668, ...,  0.07526097,
         0.06728931,  0.1058861 ],
       ...,
       [ 0.00766308,  0.10781102,  0.13686652, ...,  0.08371441,
         0.01190174,  0.12111058],
       [-0.02874381,  0.20537955,  0.11543981, ...,  0.08811261,
         0.03787484,  0.08826952],
       [ 0.12408942,  0.30591702,  0.23708522, ...,  0.1063919 ,
         0.0908693 ,  0.14098585]], dtype=float32)
```

Open-AI GPT

```
#installing necessary model
!pip install pytorch_pretrained_bert
```

```
import torch
from pytorch_pretrained_bert import OpenAIGPTTokenizer, OpenAIGPTModel
```

```
tokenizer_openai = OpenAIGPTTokenizer.from_pretrained('openai-gpt')
#Construct a GPT Tokenizer. Based on Byte-Pair-Encoding with the following
peculiarities:

model_openai = OpenAIGPTModel.from_pretrained('openai-gpt')
model_openai.eval()
print('Model Loaded')

#function to get embedding of each token
def Embedding_openai(Sentence):
  tokens = word_tokenize(Sentence)
  vectors = np.zeros((1,768))
  for word in tokens:
      subwords = tokenizer_openai.tokenize(word)
      indexed_tokens = tokenizer_openai.convert_tokens_to_ids(subwords)
      tokens_tensor = torch.tensor([indexed_tokens])
      with torch.no_grad():
          try:
            vectors += np.array(torch.mean(model_openai(tokens_tensor),1))
          except Exception as ex:
            continue
  vectors /= len(tokens)
  return vectors

# Initialize Matrix with dimension of numberof rows*vector dimension
open_ai_vec = np.zeros((df_sample.shape[0], 768))

# generating sentence embedding for each row
for iter in range(df_sample.shape[0]):
    text = df_sample.loc[iter,'description']
    open_ai_vec[iter] = Embedding_openai(text)

open_ai_vec
```

```
#output
```

```
array([[ 0.16126736,  0.14900037,  0.10306535, ...,  0.22078205,
         -0.38590393, -0.09898915],
       [ 0.17074709,  0.20849738,  0.14996684, ...,  0.21315758,
         -0.46983403,  0.02419061],
       [ 0.25158801,  0.12217634,  0.09847356, ...,  0.25541687,
         -0.44979091, -0.0174561 ],
       ...,
       [ 0.26624974,  0.15842849,  0.10565209, ...,  0.23473342,
         -0.40087843, -0.07652373],
       [ 0.22917288,  0.22115094,  0.09217898, ...,  0.18310198,
         -0.33768173, -0.16026535],
       [ 0.21503123,  0.21615047,  0.04715349, ...,  0.25044506,
         -0.42287723, -0.01473052]])
```

Step 9-6. Generate a feature vector function automatically using a selected embedding method

```
#takes input as dataframe and embedding model name as mentioned in function

def get_embed(df,model):

  if model=='Glove':
    return glove_vec
  if model=='ELMO':
    return elmo_vec
  if model=='doc2vec':
    return doc2vec_vec
  if model=='sentenceBERT':
    return sentence_embeddings_BERT
  if model=='USE':
    return embeddings_USE
  if model=='infersent':
    return infersent_embed
  if model=='Open-ai':
    return open_ai_vec
```

```
get_embed(df_sample,'ELMO')

#output
array([[ 0.0109894 , -0.16668989, -0.06553215, ...,  0.07014981,
         0.09196191,  0.04669906],
       [ 0.15317157, -0.19256656,  0.01390844, ...,  0.03459582,
         0.28029835,  0.11106762],
       [ 0.20210212, -0.13186318, -0.20647219, ..., -0.15281932,
         0.12729007,  0.17192583],

       ...,

       [ 0.29017407, -0.45098212,  0.0250571 , ..., -0.12281103,
         0.23303834,  0.15486737],
       [ 0.22871418,  0.12254314, -0.22637479, ...,  0.04150296,
         0.31900924,  0.28121516],
       [ 0.05940952,  0.01366339, -0.17502695, ...,  0.20946877,
         0.0020928 ,  0.1114894 ]], dtype=float32)
```

We hope that you are now comfortable with natural language processing. Now that the data has been cleaned and processed, and features have been created, let's jump into building applications that solve business problems.

Advanced Natural Language Processing

This chapter covers various advanced NLP techniques and leverages machine learning algorithms to extract information from text data and advanced NLP applications with a solution approach and implementation.

- Recipe 1. Noun phrase extraction

- Recipe 2. Text similarity

- Recipe 3. Parts of speech tagging

- Recipe 4. Information extraction – NER – entity recognition

- Recipe 5. Topic modeling

- Recipe 6. Text classification

- Recipe 7. Sentiment analysis

- Recipe 8. Word sense disambiguation

- Recipe 9. Speech recognition and speech to text

- Recipe 10. Text to speech

- Recipe 11. Language detection and translation

Before getting into recipes, let's understand the NLP pipeline and life cycle first. There are many concepts implemented in this book, and you might become overwhelmed by the content. To make it simpler and smoother, let's look at the flow you need to follow for an NLP solution.

© Akshay Kulkarni and Adarsha Shivananda 2021
A. Kulkarni and A. Shivananda, *Natural Language Processing Recipes*,
https://doi.org/10.1007/978-1-4842-7351-7_4

For example, let's consider customer sentiment analysis and prediction for a product or a brand, or a service.

- **Define the problem**. Understand the customer sentiment across the products.

- **Understand the depth and breadth of the problem**. Understand the customer/user sentiments across the product. Why are we doing this? What is the business impact?

- **Do data requirement brainstorming**. Have a brainstorming activity to list out all possible data points.

  - All the reviews from customers on ecommerce platforms like Amazon, Flipkart, and so on

  - Email sent by customers

  - Warranty claim forms

  - Survey data

  - Call center conversations using speech to text

  - Feedback forms

  - Social media data like Twitter, Facebook, and LinkedIn

- **Data collection**: You learned different techniques to collect the data in Chapter 1. Based on the data and the problem, you might have to incorporate different data collection methods. In this case, you can use web scraping and Twitter APIs.

- **Text preprocessing**: You know that data won't always be clean. You need to spend a significant amount of time processing it and extract insights using the methods discussed in Chapter 2.

- **Text to feature**: Text is made up of characters, and machines have a tough time understanding them. Using any of the methods you learned in previous chapters, you convert them to features that machines and algorithms can understand.

- **Machine learning/deep learning**: Machine learning and deep learning are a part of an artificial intelligence umbrella that makes systems automatically learn patterns in the data without being programmed. Most of the NLP solutions are based on this. Since text is converted to features, you can leverage machine learning or deep learning algorithms to achieve the goals like text classification and natural language generation.

- **Insights and deployment**: There is no use in building NLP solutions without proper insights being communicated to the business. Always take time to connect the dots between model/analysis output and the business, thereby creating the maximum impact.

Recipe 4-1. Extracting Noun Phrases

This recipe extracts a noun phrase from the text data (a sentence or the documents).

Problem

You want to extract a noun phrase.

Solution

Noun phrase extraction is important when you want to analyze the *who* in a sentence. Let's look at an example using TextBlob.

How It Works

Execute the following code to extract noun phrases.

```
#Import libraries
import nltk
from textblob import TextBlob

#Extract noun
blob = TextBlob("John is learning natural language processing")
for np in blob.noun_phrases:
    print(np)
```

This is the output.

```
john
natural language processing
```

Recipe 4-2. Finding Similarity Between Texts

This recipe discusses how to find the similarity between two documents or text. There are many similar metrics, like Euclidean, Cosine, and Jaccard. Applications of text similarity can be found in spelling correction, data deduplication, resume screening, search applications across various domains, and content-based recommendation system.

Here are a few of the similarity measures.

- **Cosine similarity**: Calculates the cosine of the angle between the two vectors.

- **Jaccard similarity**: The score is calculated using the intersection or union of words.

- **Jaccard Index**: (the number in both sets) / (the number in either set) * 100.

- **Levenshtein distance**: A minimal number of insertions, deletions, and replacements are required to transform string a into string b.

- **Hamming distance**: The number of positions with the same symbol in both strings. It can be defined only for strings with equal length.

You want to find the similarities between text and documents.

Solution

The simplest way to do this is by using cosine similarity from the sklearn library.

How It Works

Follow the steps in this section to compute the similarity score between text documents.

Step 2-1. Create/read the text data

Here is the data.

```
documents = (
"I like NLP",
"I am exploring NLP",
"I am a beginner in NLP",
"I want to learn NLP",
"I like advanced NLP"
)
```

Step 2-2. Find similarities

Execute the following code to find the similarity.

```
#Import libraries
from sklearn.feature_extraction.text import TfidfVectorizer
from sklearn.metrics.pairwise import cosine_similarity

#Compute tfidf : feature engineering(refer previous chapter – Recipe 3-4)

tfidf_vectorizer = TfidfVectorizer()
tfidf_matrix = tfidf_vectorizer.fit_transform(documents)

tfidf_matrix.shape

#output
(5, 10)

#compute similarity for first sentence with rest of the sentences
cosine_similarity(tfidf_matrix[0:1],tfidf_matrix)

#output
array([[ 1.        ,  0.17682765,  0.14284054,  0.13489366,  0.68374784]])
```

The first sentence and the last sentence have higher similarity compared to the rest of the sentences.

Phonetic Matching

The next version of similarity checking is phonetic matching, which roughly matches the two words or sentences and creates an alphanumeric string as an encoded version of the text or word. It is very useful for searching large text corpora, correcting spelling errors, and matching relevant names. Soundex and Metaphone are two main phonetic algorithms used for this purpose. The simplest way to do this is by using the fuzzy library.

1. Install and import the library.

```
!pip install fuzzy
import fuzzy
```

2. Run the Soundex function.

```
soundex = fuzzy.Soundex(4)
```

3. Generate the phonetic form.

```
soundex('natural')

#output
'N364'

soundex('natuaral')

#output
'N364'

soundex('language')

#output
'L52'

soundex('processing')

#output
'P625'
```

Soundex is treating natural and natuaral as the same. The phonetic code for both strings is N364. And for language and processing, it is L52 and P625, respectively.

Recipe 4-3. Tagging Part of Speech

Part of speech (POS) tagging is another crucial part of natural language processing that involves labeling the words with a part of speech such as noun, verb, adjective, and so on. POS is the base for named entity resolution, question answering, and word sense disambiguation.

Problem

You want to tag the parts of speech in a sentence.

Solution

There are two ways a tagger can be built.

- **Rule-based**: Rules created manually, which tag a word belonging to a particular POS.

- **Stochastic-based**: These algorithms capture the sequence of the words and tag the probability of the sequence using hidden Markov models.

How It Works

Again, NLTK has the best POS tagging module. `nltk.pos_tag(word)` is the function that generates the POS tagging for any given word. Use for loop and generate POS for all the words present in the document.

Step 3-1. Store the text in a variable

Here is the variable.

```
Text = "I love NLP and I will learn NLP in 2 month"
```

Step 3-2. Import NLTK for POS

Here is the code.

```
# Importing necessary packages and stopwords
import nltk
from nltk.corpus import stopwords
from nltk.tokenize import word_tokenize, sent_tokenize
stop_words = set(stopwords.words('english'))

# Tokenize the text
tokens = sent_tokenize(text)

#Generate tagging for all the tokens using loop
for i in tokens:
    words = nltk.word_tokenize(i)
    words = [w for w in words if not w in stop_words]
    #  POS-tagger.
    tags = nltk.pos_tag(words)
tags
```

These are the results.

```
[('I', 'PRP'),
 ('love', 'VBP'),
 ('NLP', 'NNP'),
 ('I', 'PRP'),
 ('learn', 'VBP'),
 ('NLP', 'RB'),
 ('2month', 'CD')]
```

The following are the short forms and explanations of POS tagging. The word *love* is VBP, which means verb, sing. present, non-3D take.

- CC coordinating conjunction

- CD cardinal digit

- DT determiner

- EX existential there (e.g., *there is* ... think of it like *there exists*)

- FW foreign word

- IN preposition/subordinating conjunction

- JJ adjective e.g: *big*

- JJR adjective, comparative e.g: *bigger*

- JJS adjective, superlative e.g: *biggest*

- LS list marker 1)

- MD modal could, will

- NN noun, singular *desk*

- NNS noun plural *desks*

- NNP proper noun, singular *Harrison*

- NNPS proper noun, plural *Americans*

- PDT predeterminer *all the kids*

- POS possessive ending parents

- PRP personal pronoun I, he, she

- PRP$ possessive pronoun my, his, hers

- RB adverb very, silently

- RBR adverb, comparative better

- RBS adverb, superlative best

- RP particle give up

- TO to go *to* the store

- UH interjection

- VB verb, base form take

- VBD verb, past tense *took*

- VBG verb, gerund/present participle *taking*

- VBN verb, past participle *taken*

- VBP verb, sing, present. non-3D *take*

- VBZ verb, 3rd person sing. present *takes*

- WDT wh-determiner which

- WP wh-pronoun who, what

- WP$ possessive wh-pronoun whose

- WRB wh-adverb where, when

Recipe 4-4. Extracting Entities from Text

This recipe discusses how to identify and extract entities from the text, which is called *named entity recognition*. Multiple libraries perform this task, like NLTK chunker, Stanford NER, spaCy, OpenNLP, and NeuroNER. And there are many APIs, like Watson NLU, AlchemyAPI, NERD, Google Cloud Natural Language API, and many more.

Problem

You want to identify and extract entities from text.

Solution

The simplest way to do this is by using the ne_chunk from NLTK or spaCy.

How It Works

Follow the steps in this section to perform NER.

Step 4-1. Read/create the text data

This is the text.

```
sent = "John is studying at Stanford University in California"
```

Step 4-2. Extract the entities

Execute the following code.

Using NLTK

```
#import libraries
import nltk

from nltk import ne_chunk
from nltk import word_tokenize

#NER
ne_chunk(nltk.pos_tag(word_tokenize(sent)), binary=False)

#output

Tree('S', [Tree('PERSON', [('John', 'NNP')]), ('is', 'VBZ'), ('studying',
'VBG'), ('at', 'IN'), Tree('ORGANIZATION', [('Stanford', 'NNP'),
('University', 'NNP')]), ('in', 'IN'), Tree('GPE', [('California', 'NNP')])])
```

```
Here "John" is tagged as "PERSON"
"Stanford" as "ORGANIZATION"
"California" as "GPE". Geopolitical entity, i.e. countries, cities, states.
```

Using spaCy

```
import spacy
nlp = spacy.load('en')

# Read/create a sentence
doc = nlp(u'Apple is ready to launch new phone worth $10000 in New york
time square ')

for ent in doc.ents:
    print(ent.text, ent.start_char, ent.end_char, ent.label_)

#output

Apple 0 5 ORG
10000 42 47 MONEY
New york 51 59 GPE
```

According to the output, Apple is an organization, 10000 is money, and New York is a place. The results are accurate and can be used in any NLP application.

Recipe 4-5. Extracting Topics from Text

This recipe discusses how to identify topics from the document. For example , there is an online library with multiple departments based on the kind/genre of the book. You look at unique keywords/topics to decide which department this book likely belongs to, and place it accordingly. In these kinds of situations, topic modeling would come handy. It is called *document tagging and clustering*.

Problem

You want to extract or identify topics from a document.

Solution

The simplest way is to use the gensim library.

How It Works

Follow the steps in this section to identify topics within documents using genism.

Step 5-1. Create the text data

Here is the text.

```
doc1 = "I am learning NLP, it is very interesting and exciting. it includes
        machine learning and deep learning"
doc2 = "My father is a data scientist and he is nlp expert"
doc3 = "My sister has good exposure into android development"

doc_complete = [doc1, doc2, doc3]
doc_complete

#output
['I am learning NLP, it is very interesting and exciting. it includes
machine learning and deep learning',
 'My father is a data scientist and he is nlp expert',
 'My sister has good exposure into android development']
```

Step 5-2. Clean and preprocess the data

Next, let's clean it up.

```
# Install and import libraries

!pip install gensim
from nltk.corpus import stopwords
from nltk.stem.wordnet import WordNetLemmatizer
import string

# Text preprocessing as discussed in chapter 2

stop = set(stopwords.words('english'))
exclude = set(string.punctuation)
lemma = WordNetLemmatizer()
def clean(doc):
    stop_free = " ".join([i for i in doc.lower().split() if i not in stop])
    punc_free = "".join(ch for ch in stop_free if ch not in exclude)
    normalized = " ".join(lemma.lemmatize(word) for word in punc_free.split())
    return normalized

doc_clean = [clean(doc).split() for doc in doc_complete]

doc_clean

#output
[['learning',
  'nlp',
  'interesting',
  'exciting',
  'includes',
  'machine',
  'learning',
  'deep',
  'learning'],
 ['father', 'data', 'scientist', 'nlp', 'expert'],
 ['sister', 'good', 'exposure', 'android', 'development']]
```

Step 5-3. Prepare the document term matrix

The following is the code.

```
# Importing gensim

import gensim
from gensim import corpora

# Creating the term dictionary of our corpus, where every unique term is
assigned an index.

dictionary = corpora.Dictionary(doc_clean)

# Converting a list of documents (corpus) into Document-Term Matrix using
dictionary prepared above.

doc_term_matrix = [dictionary.doc2bow(doc) for doc in doc_clean]

doc_term_matrix

#output
[[(0, 1), (1, 1), (2, 1), (3, 1), (4, 3), (5, 1), (6, 1)],
 [(6, 1), (7, 1), (8, 1), (9, 1), (10, 1)],
 [(11, 1), (12, 1), (13, 1), (14, 1), (15, 1)]]
```

Step 5-4. Create the LDA model

The final part creates the LDA model.

```
# Creating the object for LDA model using gensim library
Lda = gensim.models.ldamodel.LdaModel

# Running and Training LDA model on the document term matrix for 3 topics.
ldamodel = Lda(doc_term_matrix, num_topics=3, id2word = dictionary, passes=50)

# Results
print(ldamodel.print_topics())

#output
[(0, '0.063*"nlp" + 0.063*"father" + 0.063*"data" + 0.063*"scientist" +
0.063*"expert" + 0.063*"good" + 0.063*"exposure" + 0.063*"development" +
```

```
0.063*"android" + 0.063*"sister"'), (1, '0.232*"learning" + 0.093*"nlp" +
0.093*"deep" + 0.093*"includes" + 0.093*"interesting" + 0.093*"machine" +
0.093*"exciting" + 0.023*"scientist" + 0.023*"data" + 0.023*"father"'), (2,
'0.087*"sister" + 0.087*"good" + 0.087*"exposure" + 0.087*"development"
+ 0.087*"android" + 0.087*"father" + 0.087*"scientist" + 0.087*"data" +
0.087*"expert" + 0.087*"nlp"')]
```

All the weights associated with the topics from the sentence seem almost similar. You can perform this on huge documents to extract significant topics. The whole idea to implement this on sample data is to make you familiar with it, and you can use the same code snippet to perform on the huge data for significant results and insights.

Recipe 4-6. Classifying Text

Text classification automatically classifies text documents based on pre-trained categories. It has the following applications.

- Sentiment analysis
- Document classification
- Spam/ham mail classification
- Complaint classification
- Product classification
- Fake news detection

Problem

Spam/ham classification using machine learning.

Solution

Gmail has a folder called Spam. It classifies your emails into spam and ham so that you don't have to read unnecessary emails.

How It Works

Follow the step-by-step method to build the classifier.

Step 6-1. Collect and understand the data

Please download data from www.kaggle.com/uciml/sms-spam-collection
-dataset#spam.csv and save it in your working directory.

```
#Read the data
Email_Data = pd.read_csv("spam.csv",encoding ='latin1')
```

```
#Data undestanding
Email_Data.columns
```

```
#output
Index(['v1', 'v2', 'Unnamed: 2', 'Unnamed: 3', 'Unnamed: 4'], dtype="object")
```

```
Email_Data = Email_Data[['v1', 'v2']]
Email_Data = Email_Data.rename(columns={"v1":"Target", "v2":"Email"})
```

```
Email_Data.head()
```

```
#output
    Target   Email
0      ham   Go until jurong point, crazy.. Available only ...
1      ham   Ok lar... Joking wif u oni...
2     spam   Free entry in 2 a wkly comp to win FA Cup fina...
3      ham   U dun say so early hor... U c already then say...
4      ham   Nah I don't think he goes to usf, he lives aro...
```

Step 6-2. Text processing and feature engineering

The following is the code.

```
#import
import numpy as np
import pandas as pd
import matplotlib.pyplot as plt
import string
```

```python
from nltk.stem import SnowballStemmer
from nltk.corpus import stopwords
from sklearn.feature_extraction.text import TfidfVectorizer
from sklearn.model_selection import train_test_split
import os
from textblob import TextBlob
from nltk.stem import PorterStemmer
from textblob import Word
from sklearn.feature_extraction.text import CountVectorizer,TfidfVectorizer
import sklearn.feature_extraction.text as text
from sklearn import model_selection, preprocessing, linear_model, naive_
bayes, metrics, svm

#pre processing steps like lower case, stemming and lemmatization

Email_Data['Email'] = Email_Data['Email'].apply(lambda x: " ".join(x.
                      lower() for x in x.split()))
stop = stopwords.words('english')
Email_Data['Email'] = Email_Data['Email'].apply(lambda x: "
                      ".join(x for x in x.split() if x not in stop))
st = PorterStemmer()
Email_Data['Email'] = Email_Data['Email'].apply(lambda x: "
                      ".join([st.stem(word) for word in x.split()]))
Email_Data['Email'] = Email_Data['Email'].apply(lambda x: " ".join([Word
                      (word).lemmatize() for word in x.split()]))

Email_Data.head()

#output
  Target                                         Email
0    ham  go jurong point, crazy.. avail bugi n great wo...
1    ham                          ok lar... joke wif u oni...
2   spam free entri 2 wkli comp win fa cup final tkt 21...
3    ham            u dun say earli hor... u c alreadi say...
4    ham              nah think goe usf, live around though

#Splitting data into train and validation
```

```
train_x, valid_x, train_y, valid_y = model_selection.train_test_
split(Email_Data['Email'], Email_Data['Target'])

# TFIDF feature generation for a maximum of 5000 features

encoder = preprocessing.LabelEncoder()
train_y = encoder.fit_transform(train_y)
valid_y = encoder.fit_transform(valid_y)

tfidf_vect = TfidfVectorizer(analyzer='word', token_pattern=r'\w{1,}',
            max_features=5000)

tfidf_vect.fit(Email_Data['Email'])
xtrain_tfidf =  tfidf_vect.transform(train_x)
xvalid_tfidf =  tfidf_vect.transform(valid_x)

xtrain_tfidf.data

#output
array([0.39933971, 0.36719906, 0.60411187, ..., 0.36682939, 0.30602539,
0.38290119])
```

Step 6-3. Model training

This is the generalized function for training any given model.

```
def train_model(classifier, feature_vector_train, label,
feature_vector_valid, is_neural_net=False):
    # fit the training dataset on the classifier
    classifier.fit(feature_vector_train, label)
    # predict the labels on validation dataset
    predictions = classifier.predict(feature_vector_valid)
    return metrics.accuracy_score(predictions, valid_y)

# Naive Bayes trainig
accuracy = train_model(naive_bayes.MultinomialNB(alpha=0.2), xtrain_tfidf,
train_y, xvalid_tfidf)
print ("Accuracy: ", accuracy)
```

```
#output
Accuracy:  0.985642498205

# Linear Classifier on Word Level TF IDF Vectors
accuracy = train_model(linear_model.LogisticRegression(), xtrain_tfidf,
          train_y, xvalid_tfidf)
print ("Accuracy: ", accuracy)

#output
Accuracy:  0.970567121321
```

The naive Bayes classifier provides better results than the linear classifier. You should try a few other classifiers and then choose the best one.

Recipe 4-7. Carrying Out Sentiment Analysis

This recipe discusses the sentiment of a particular sentence or statement. Sentiment analysis is one of the widely used techniques across the industries to understand the sentiments of the customers/users around the products/services. Sentiment analysis gives the sentiment score of a sentence/statement tending toward positive or negative.

Problem

You want to do a sentiment analysis.

Solution

The simplest way is to use TextBlob or VADER.

How It Works

Follow the steps in this section to do sentiment analysis using TextBlob. It has two metrics.

- Polarity lies in the range of [–1,1], where 1 means a positive statement and –1 means a negative statement.

- Subjectivity [0,1] is an opinion and not factual information.

Step 7-1. Create the sample data

Here is the sample data.

```
review = "I like this phone. screen quality and camera  clarity is really good."
review2 = "This tv is not good. Bad quality, no clarity, worst experience"
```

Step 7-2. Clean and preprocess the data

Refer to Chapter 2, Recipe 2-10, for this step.

Step 7-3. Get the sentiment scores

Use a pre-trained TextBlob to get the sentiment scores.

```
#import libraries
from textblob import TextBlob

#TextBlob has a pre trained sentiment prediction model
blob = TextBlob(review)
blob.sentiment

#output
Sentiment(polarity=0.7, subjectivity=0.6000000000000001)
```

It seems like a very positive review.

```
#now lets look at the sentiment of review2
blob = TextBlob(review2)
blob.sentiment

#output
Sentiment(polarity=-0.6833333333333332, subjectivity=0.7555555555555555)
```

This is a negative review since the polarity is –0.68.

Note   A real-time use case on sentiment analysis with an end-to-end
implementation is covered in Recipe 5-2 in the next chapter.

Recipe 4-8. Disambiguating Text

Ambiguity arises due to the different meanings of words in a different context.

For example,

```
Text1 = 'I went to the bank to deposit my money'
Text2 = 'The river bank was full of dead fish'
```

In the texts, the word bank has different meanings based on the context of the sentence.

Problem

You want to understand disambiguating word sense.

Solution

The Lesk algorithm is one of the best algorithms for word sense disambiguation. Let's look at how to solve it using the pywsd and nltk packages.

How It Works

The following are the steps to achieve the results.

Step 8-1. Import libraries

First, import the libraries.

```
#Install pywsd

!pip install pywsd

#Import functions

from nltk.corpus import wordnet as wn
from nltk.stem import PorterStemmer
from itertools import chain
from pywsd.lesk import simple_lesk
```

Step 8-2. Disambiguate word sense

Here is the code.

```
# Sentences

bank_sents = ['I went to the bank to deposit my money',
'The river bank was full of dead fishes']

# calling the lesk function and printing results for both the sentences

print ("Context-1:", bank_sents[0])
answer = simple_lesk(bank_sents[0],'bank')
print ("Sense:", answer)
print ("Definition : ", answer.definition())

print ("Context-2:", bank_sents[1])
answer = simple_lesk(bank_sents[1],'bank','n')
print ("Sense:", answer)
print ("Definition : ", answer.definition())

#Result:
Context-1: I went to the bank to deposit my money
Sense: Synset('depository_financial_institution.n.01')
Definition :  a financial institution that accepts deposits and channels
the money into lending activities

Context-2: The river bank was full of dead fishes
Sense: Synset('bank.n.01')
Definition :  sloping land (especially the slope beside a body of water)
```

Observe that in context-1, "bank" is a financial institution, but in context-2, "bank" is sloping land.

Recipe 4-9. Converting Speech to Text

Converting speech to text is a very useful NLP technique.

Problem

You want to convert speech to text.

Solution

The simplest way is to use speech recognition and PyAudio.

How It Works

Follow the steps in this section to implement speech to text.

Step 9-1. Define the business problem

Interaction with machines is trending toward the voice, which is the usual way of human communication. Popular examples are Apple Siri, Amazon Alexa, and Google Home.

Step 9-2. Install and import necessary libraries

Here are the libraries.

```
!pip install SpeechRecognition
!pip install PyAudio

import speech_recognition as sr
```

Step 9-3. Run the code

Now after you run the following code snippet, whatever you say on the microphone (using the recognize_google function) is converted into text.

```
r=sr.Recognizer()

with sr.Microphone() as source:
    print("Please say something")
    audio = r.listen(source)
    print("Time over, thanks")
try:
    print("I think you said: "+r.recognize_google(audio));
```

```
except:
    pass;
```

```
#output
Please say something
Time over, thanks
I think you said: I am learning natural language processing
```

This code works with the default English language. If you speak another language, for example, Hindi, the text is interpreted in English, as follows.

```
#code snippet
r=sr.Recognizer()

with sr.Microphone() as source:
    print("Please say something")
    audio = r.listen(source)
    print("Time over, thanks")

try:
    print("I think you said: "+r.recognize_google(audio));
except:
    pass;
```

```
#output
Please say something
Time over, thanks
I think you said: aapka naam kya hai
```

If you want the text to appear in the spoken language, please run the following code snippet. A minor change is made to recognize_google -language ('hi-IN', which means Hindi).

```
#code snippet
r=sr.Recognizer()

with sr.Microphone() as source:
    print("Please say something")
    audio = r.listen(source)
    print("Time over, thanks")
```

```
try:
    print("I think you said: "+r.recognize_google(audio, language ='hi-IN'));
except sr.UnknownValueError:
    print("Google Speech Recognition could not understand audio")
except sr.RequestError as e:
    print("Could not request results from Google Speech Recognition
    service; {0}".format(e))
except:
    pass;
```

Recipe 4-10. Converting Text to Speech

Converting text to speech is another useful NLP technique.

Problem

You want to convert text to speech.

Solution

The simplest way is to use the gTTs library.

How It Works

Follow the steps in this section to implement text to speech.

Step 10-1. Install and import necessary libraries

Here are the libraries.

```
!pip install gTTS
```

```
from gtts import gTTS
```

Step 10-2. Run the code with the gTTs function

Now after you run the following code snippet, whatever you input in the text parameter gets converted into audio.

```
#chooses the language, English('en')

convert = gTTS(text='I like this NLP book', lang="en", slow=False)

# Saving the converted audio in a mp3 file named
myobj.save("audio.mp3")

#output
Please play the audio.mp3 file saved in your local machine to hear the audio.
```

Recipe 4-11. Translating Speech

Language detection and translation.

Problem

Whenever you try to analyze data from blogs hosted across the globe, especially websites from countries like China, where the Chinese language is predominant, analyzing such data or performing NLP tasks on such data would be difficult. That's where language translation comes to the rescue. You want to translate one language to another.

Solution

The easiest way to is to use the goslate library.

How It Works

Follow the steps in this section to implement language translation in Python.

Step 11-1. Install and import necessary libraries

Here are the libraries.

```
!pip install goslate
import goslate
```

Step 11-2. Input text

Enter the following simple phrase.

```
text = "Bonjour le monde"
```

Step 11-3. Run the goslate function

Run the translation function.

```
gs = goslate.Goslate()
translatedText = gs.translate(text,'en')
```

```
print(translatedText)
```

```
#output
Hi world
```

Note   You can also use the polyglot library. It has various multilingual applications and supports more than 100 languages in NLP tasks, such as language detection, tokenization, NER, POS tagging, and sentiment analysis.

Well, it feels accomplished. You have implemented many advanced NLP applications and techniques. But that is not all, folks. There are more interesting chapters ahead, where you look at the industrial applications around NLP, their solution approach, and end-to-end implementation.

CHAPTER 5

Implementing Industry Applications

This chapter implements end-to-end solutions for a few of the industry applications around NLP.

- Recipe 1. Consumer complaint classification

- Recipe 2. Customer reviews sentiment prediction

- Recipe 3. Data stitching using record linkage

- Recipe 4. Text summarization for subject notes

- Recipe 5. Document clustering

- Recipe 6. Search engines and learning to rank

- Recipe 7. Fake news detection

- Recipe 8. Movie genre tagging

We believe that after four chapters, you are comfortable with the concepts of natural language processing and ready to solve some business problems. You need to keep all four chapters in mind and think of approaches to solve these problems at hand. It can be one concept or a series of concepts leveraged to build applications.

So, let's go through them one by one to better understand end-to-end implementation.

Recipe 5-1. Implementing Multiclass Classification

Let's understand how to do multiclass classification for text data in Python through solving consumer complaint classifications for the finance industry.

© Akshay Kulkarni and Adarsha Shivananda 2021
A. Kulkarni and A. Shivananda, *Natural Language Processing Recipes*,
https://doi.org/10.1007/978-1-4842-7351-7_5

Problem

Each week the US Consumer Financial Protection Bureau (www.consumerfinance.gov) sends thousands of consumers' complaints about financial products and services to companies for a response. You want to classify those consumer complaints into the product category it belongs to using the description of the complaint.

Solution

The goal of the project is to classify the complaint into a specific product category. Since it has multiple categories, it becomes a multiclass classification that can be solved through many machine learning algorithms.

Once the algorithm is in place, you can easily categorize it whenever there is a new complaint and be redirected to the concerned person. This saves a lot of time because you minimize the human intervention to decide whom this complaint should go to.

How It Works

Let's explore the data and build classification problems using many machine learning algorithms and see which one gives better results.

Step 1-1. Get the data from Kaggle

Go to www.kaggle.com/subhassing/exploring-consumer-complaint-data/data and download the data.

Step 1-2. Import the libraries

Here are the libraries.

```
import numpy as np
import pandas as pd
import matplotlib.pyplot as plt
import string
from nltk.stem import SnowballStemmer
from nltk.corpus import stopwords
from sklearn.feature_extraction.text import TfidfVectorizer
```

```
from sklearn.model_selection import train_test_split
import os
from textblob import TextBlob
from nltk.stem import PorterStemmer
from textblob import Word
from sklearn.feature_extraction.text import CountVectorizer,TfidfVectorizer
import sklearn.feature_extraction.text as text
from sklearn import model_selection, preprocessing, linear_model, naive_
bayes, metrics, svm
from sklearn.naive_bayes import MultinomialNB
from sklearn.linear_model import LogisticRegression
from sklearn.ensemble import RandomForestClassifier
from sklearn.svm import LinearSVC
from sklearn.model_selection import cross_val_score
from io import StringIO
import seaborn as sns
```

Step 1-3. Import the data

Import the data that was downloaded in the last step.

```
Data = pd.read_csv("/Consumer_Complaints.csv",encoding='latin-1')
```

Step 1-4. Analyze the date

Let's analyze the columns.

```
Data.dtypes
date_received                    object
product                          object
sub_product                      object
issue                            object
sub_issue                        object
consumer_complaint_narrative     object
company_public_response          object
company                          object
state                            object
```

```
zipcode                          object
tags                             object
consumer_consent_provided        object
submitted_via                    object
date_sent_to_company             object
company_response_to_consumer     object
timely_response                  object
consumer_disputed?               object
complaint_id                      int64
```

```
# Selecting required columns and rows
Data = Data[['product', 'consumer_complaint_narrative']]
Data = Data[pd.notnull(Data['consumer_complaint_narrative'])]
```

```
# See top 5 rows
Data.head()
                product                       consumer_complaint_narrative
190126  Debt collection    XXXX has claimed I owe them {$27.00} for XXXX ...
190135     Consumer Loan    Due to inconsistencies in the amount owed that...
190155          Mortgage    In XX/XX/XXXX my wages that I earned at my job...
190207          Mortgage    I have an open and current mortgage with Chase...
190208          Mortgage    XXXX was submitted XX/XX/XXXX. At the time I s...
```

```
# Factorizing the category column
Data['category_id'] = Data['product'].factorize()[0]
Data.head()
                product     consumer_complaint_narrative    \
190126  Debt collection    XXXX has claimed I owe them {$27.00} for XXXX ...
190135     Consumer Loan    Due to inconsistencies in the amount owed that...

        category_id
190126            0
190135            1
```

```
# Check the distriution of complaints by category
Data.groupby('product').consumer_complaint_narrative.count()
product
```

```
Bank account or service    5711
Consumer Loan              3678
Credit card                7929
Credit reporting           12526
Debt collection            17552
Money transfers            666
Mortgage                   14919
Other financial service    110
Payday loan                726
Prepaid card               861
Student loan               2128
```

```
# Lets plot it and see
fig = plt.figure(figsize=(8,6))
Data.groupby('product').consumer_complaint_narrative.count().
plot.bar(ylim=0)
plt.show()
```

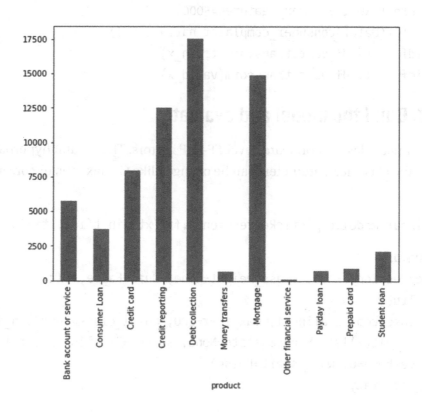

Debt collection and mortgage have the highest number of complaints registered.

Step 1-5. Split the data

Split the data into train and validation.

```
train_x, valid_x, train_y, valid_y = model_selection.train_test_
split(Data['consumer_complaint_narrative'], Data['product'])
```

Step 1-6. Use TF-IDF for feature engineering

Create TF-IDF vectors, as discussed in Chapter 3. Here we consider maximum features to be 5000.

```
encoder = preprocessing.LabelEncoder()
train_y = encoder.fit_transform(train_y)
valid_y = encoder.fit_transform(valid_y)

tfidf_vect = TfidfVectorizer(analyzer='word',
token_pattern=r'\w{1,}', max_features=5000)
tfidf_vect.fit(Data['consumer_complaint_narrative'])
xtrain_tfidf =  tfidf_vect.transform(train_x)
xvalid_tfidf =  tfidf_vect.transform(valid_x)
```

Step 1-7. Build the model and evaluate

Let's build a linear classifier on word-level TF-IDF vectors. The default hyperparameters are used for the classifier. Parameters can be changed like C, max_iter, or solver to obtain better results.

```
model = linear_model.LogisticRegression().fit(xtrain_tfidf, train_y)

# Model summary
LogisticRegression(C=1.0, class_weight=None, dual=False, fit_
intercept=True,
          intercept_scaling=1, max_iter=100, multi_class="ovr", n_jobs=1,
          penalty='l2', random_state=None, solver="liblinear", tol=0.0001,
          verbose=0, warm_start=False)
# Checking accuracy
```

```
accuracy = metrics.accuracy_score(model.predict(xvalid_tfidf), valid_y)
print ("Accuracy: ", accuracy)
Accuracy:  0.845048497186
# Classification report
print(metrics.classification_report(valid_y, model.predict(xvalid_
tfidf),target_names=Data['product'].unique()))
```

	precision	recall	f1-score	support
Debt collection	0.81	0.79	0.80	1414
Consumer Loan	0.81	0.56	0.66	942
Mortgage	0.80	0.82	0.81	1997
Credit card	0.85	0.85	0.85	3162
Credit reporting	0.82	0.90	0.86	4367
Student loan	0.77	0.48	0.59	151
Bank account or service	0.92	0.96	0.94	3717
Payday loan	0.00	0.00	0.00	26
Money transfers	0.76	0.23	0.35	172
Other financial service	0.77	0.57	0.65	209
Prepaid card	0.92	0.76	0.83	545
avg / total	0.84	0.85	0.84	16702

```
#confusion matrix
conf_mat = confusion_matrix(valid_y, model.predict(xvalid_tfidf))
# Vizualizing confusion matrix
category_id_df = Data[['product', 'category_id']].drop_duplicates().sort_
values('category_id')
category_to_id = dict(category_id_df.values)
id_to_category = dict(category_id_df[['category_id', 'product']].values)

fig, ax = plt.subplots(figsize=(8,6))
sns.heatmap(conf_mat, annot=True, fmt="d", cmap="BuPu",
            xticklabels=category_id_df[['product']].values,
            yticklabels=category_id_df[['product']].values)
plt.ylabel('Actual')
plt.xlabel('Predicted')
plt.show()
```

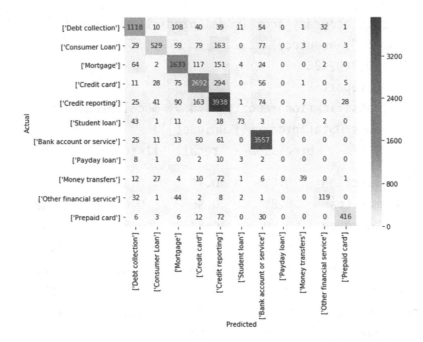

The accuracy of 85% is good for a baseline model. Precision and recall look pretty good across the categories except for "Payday loan." If you look for Payload loan, most of the wrong predictions are Debt collection and Credit card, which might be because of the smaller number of samples in that category. It also sounds like it's a subcategory of a credit card. You can add these samples to any other group to make the model more stable. Let's see what prediction looks like for one example.

```
# Prediction example
texts = ["This company refuses to provide me verification and validation of
        debt"+ "per my right under the FDCPA. I do not believe this debt is
        mine."]
text_features = tfidf_vect.transform(texts)
predictions = model.predict(text_features)
print(texts)
print("  - Predicted as: '{}'".format(id_to_category[predictions[0]]))

Result :
['This company refuses to provide me verification and validation of debt
per my right under the FDCPA. I do not believe this debt is mine.']
  - Predicted as: 'Credit reporting'
```

To increase the accuracy, you can do the following things.

- Reiterate the process with different algorithms like random forest, SVM, GBM, neural networks, naive Bayes.

- Deep learning techniques like RNN and LSTM (discussed in Chapter 6) can also be used.

- In each of these algorithms, there are so many parameters to be tuned to get better results. It can be easily done through grid search, which tries all possible combinations and gives the best out.

Recipe 5-2. Implementing Sentiment Analysis

This recipe implements, end to end, a popular NLP industrial application: sentiment analysis. From a business standpoint, it is very important to understand how customer feedback is on the products/services they offer to improvise on the products/service for customer satisfaction.

Problem

You want to implement sentiment analysis.

Solution

The simplest way is to use TextBlob or the vaderSentiment library. Since you have already used TextBlob, now let's use Vader.

How It Works

Follow the steps in this section to implement sentiment analysis on the business problem.

Step 2-1. Define the business problem

Understand how products are doing in the market. How are customers reacting to a particular product? What is the consumer's sentiment across products? Many more questions like these can be answered using sentiment analysis.

Step 2-2. Identify potential data sources and extract insights

We have a dataset for Amazon food reviews. Let's use that data and extract insight out of it. You can download the data from www.kaggle.com/snap/amazon-fine-food-reviews.

```python
# Import necessary libraries
import numpy as np
import pandas as pd
import matplotlib.pyplot as plt
%matplotlib inline

#Read the data
df = pd.read_csv('Reviews.csv')

# Look at the top 5 rows of the data
df.head(5)

#output
```

	Id	ProductId	UserId	ProfileName	HelpfulnessNumerator	HelpfulnessDenominator	Score	Time	Summary	Text
0	1	B001E4KFG0	A3SGXH7AUHU8GW	delmartian	1	1	5	1303862400	Good Quality Dog Food	I have bought several of the Vitality canned d...
1	2	B00813GRG4	A1D87F6ZCVE5NK	dll pa	0	0	1	1346976000	Not as Advertised	Product arrived labeled as Jumbo Salted Peanut...
2	3	B000LQOCH0	ABXLMWJIXXAIN	Natalia Corres "Natalia Corres"	1	1	4	1219017600	"Delight" says it all	This is a confection that has been around a fe...
3	4	B000UA0QIQ	A395BORC6FGVXV	Karl	3	3	2	1307923200	Cough Medicine	If you are looking for the secret ingredient i...
4	5	B006K2ZZ7K	A1UQRSCLF8GW1T	Michael D. Bigham "M. Wassir"	0	0	5	1350777600	Great taffy	Great taffy at a great price. There was a wid...

```
# Understand the data types of the columns
df.info()

# Output
Data columns (total 10 columns):
Id                      5 non-null int64
ProductId               5 non-null object
UserId                  5 non-null object
ProfileName             5 non-null object
HelpfulnessNumerator    5 non-null int64
HelpfulnessDenominator  5 non-null int64
Score                   5 non-null int64
Time                    5 non-null int64
Summary                 5 non-null object
Text                    5 non-null object
dtypes: int64(5), object(5)
# Looking at the summary of the reviews.
df.Summary.head(5)

# Output
0      Good Quality Dog Food
1          Not as Advertised
2       "Delight" says it all
3             Cough Medicine
4                 Great taffy

# Looking at the description of the reviews
df.Text.head(5)

#output
0    I have bought several of the Vitality canned d...
1    Product arrived labeled as Jumbo Salted Peanut...
2    This is a confection that has been around a fe...
3    If you are looking for the secret ingredient i...
4    Great taffy at a great price.  There was a wid...
```

Step 2-3. Preprocess the data

You know the importance of this step. Perform a preprocessing task, as discussed in Chapter 2.

```python
# Import libraries
from nltk.corpus import stopwords
from textblob import TextBlob
from textblob import Word

# Lower casing and removing punctuations
df['Text'] = df['Text'].apply(lambda x: " ".join(x.lower() for x in
x.split()))
df['Text'] = df['Text'].str.replace('[^\w\s]','')
df.Text.head(5)
# Output
0    i have bought several of the vitality canned d...
1    product arrived labeled as jumbo salted peanut...
2    this is a confection that has been around a fe...
3    if you are looking for the secret ingredient i...
4    great taffy at a great price there was a wide ...

# Removal of stop words
stop = stopwords.words('english')
df['Text'] = df['Text'].apply(lambda x: " ".join(x for x in x.split() if x
not in stop))
df.Text.head(5)
# Output
0    bought several vitality canned dog food produc...
1    product arrived labeled jumbo salted peanutsth...
2    confection around centuries light pillowy citr...
3    looking secret ingredient robitussin believe f...
4    great taffy great price wide assortment yummy ...

# Spelling correction
df['Text'] = df['Text'].apply(lambda x: str(TextBlob(x).correct()))
df.Text.head(5)
# Output
```

```
0    bought several vitality canned dog food produc...
1    product arrived labelled lumbo halted peanutst...
2    connection around centuries light pillow citie...
3    looking secret ingredient robitussin believe f...
4    great staff great price wide assortment mummy ...

# Lemmatization
df['Text'] = df['Text'].apply(lambda x: " ".join([Word(word).lemmatize()
for word in x.split()]))
df.Text.head(5)
# Output
0    bought several vitality canned dog food produc...
1    product arrived labelled lumbo halted peanutst...
2    connection around century light pillow city ge...
3    looking secret ingredient robitussin believe f...
4    great staff great price wide assortment mummy ...
```

Step 2-4. Analyze data

This step is not connected anywhere in predicting sentiments; what we are trying to do here is to dig deeper into the data and understand it.

```
# Create a new data frame "reviews" to perform exploratory data analysis
upon that
reviews = df
# Dropping null values
reviews.dropna(inplace=True)

# The histogram reveals this dataset is highly unbalanced towards high
rating.
reviews.Score.hist(bins=5,grid=False)
plt.show()
print(reviews.groupby('Score').count().Id)
```

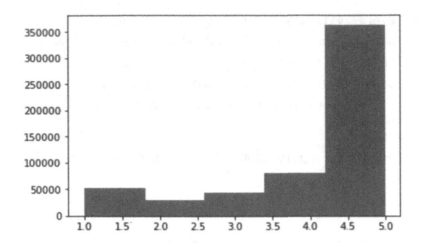

```
# To make it balanced data, we sampled each score by the lowest n-count
from above. (i.e. 29743 reviews scored as '2')
score_1 = reviews[reviews['Score'] == 1].sample(n=29743)
score_2 = reviews[reviews['Score'] == 2].sample(n=29743)
score_3 = reviews[reviews['Score'] == 3].sample(n=29743)
score_4 = reviews[reviews['Score'] == 4].sample(n=29743)
score_5 = reviews[reviews['Score'] == 5].sample(n=29743)
# Here we recreate a 'balanced' dataset.
reviews_sample = pd.concat([score_1,score_2,score_3,score_4,score_5],axis=0)
reviews_sample.reset_index(drop=True,inplace=True)
```

You can use this dataset if you are training your own sentiment classifier from scratch. And to do this, you can follow the same steps as in text classification (Recipe 5-1). Here our target variable would be positive, negative, and neutral created using score.

- Score <= 2: Negative

- Score = 3: Neutral

- Score > =4: Positive

Having said that, let's get back to our exploratory data analysis.

```
# Printing count by 'Score' to check dataset is now balanced.
print(reviews_sample.groupby('Score').count().Id)
# Output
Score
```

```
1      29743
2      29743
3      29743
4      29743
5      29743
# Let's build a word cloud looking at the 'Summary' text
from wordcloud import WordCloud
from wordcloud import STOPWORDS
# Wordcloud function's input needs to be a single string of text.
# Here I'm concatenating all Summaries into a single string.
# similarly you can build for Text column
reviews_str = reviews_sample.Summary.str.cat()
wordcloud = WordCloud(background_color='white').generate(reviews_str)
plt.figure(figsize=(10,10))
plt.imshow(wordcloud,interpolation='bilinear')
plt.axis("off")
plt.show()
```

```
# Now let's split the data into Negative (Score is 1 or 2) and Positive (4
or #5) Reviews.
negative_reviews = reviews_sample[reviews_sample['Score'].isin([1,2]) ]
positive_reviews = reviews_sample[reviews_sample['Score'].isin([4,5]) ]
# Transform to single string
negative_reviews_str = negative_reviews.Summary.str.cat()
positive_reviews_str = positive_reviews.Summary.str.cat()
# Create wordclouds
```

```
wordcloud_negative = WordCloud(background_color='white').generate
                    (negative_reviews_str)
wordcloud_positive = WordCloud(background_color='white').generate
                    (positive_reviews_str)
# Plot
fig = plt.figure(figsize=(10,10))
ax1 = fig.add_subplot(211)
ax1.imshow(wordcloud_negative,interpolation='bilinear')
ax1.axis("off")
ax1.set_title('Reviews with Negative Scores',fontsize=20)
```

```
ax2 = fig.add_subplot(212)
ax2.imshow(wordcloud_positive,interpolation='bilinear')
ax2.axis("off")
ax2.set_title('Reviews with Positive Scores',fontsize=20)
plt.show()
#output
```

Step 2-5. Use a pre-trained model

This step is not required because we are not building the model from scratch; rather, we use the pre-trained model from the vaderSentiment library.

If you want to build the model from scratch, you can leverage the positive and negative classes created while exploring as a target variable and then training the model. You can follow the same steps as text classification explained in Recipe 5-1 to build a sentiment classifier from scratch.

Step 2-6. Do sentiment analysis

In sentiment analysis, pre-trained model takes the input from the text description and outputs the sentiment score ranging from –1 to +1 for each sentence.

```
#Importing required libraries
import pandas as pd
import numpy as np
import matplotlib.pyplot as plt
%matplotlib inline
import seaborn as sns
import re
import os
import sys
```

```python
import ast
plt.style.use('fivethirtyeight')
# Function for getting the sentiment
cp = sns.color_palette()
from vaderSentiment.vaderSentiment import SentimentIntensityAnalyzer
analyzer = SentimentIntensityAnalyzer()

# Generating sentiment for all the sentence present in the dataset
emptyline=[]
for row in df['Text']:
    vs=analyzer.polarity_scores(row)
    emptyline.append(vs)

# Creating new dataframe with sentiments
df_sentiments=pd.DataFrame(emptyline)
df_sentiments.head(5)

# Output
      compound    neg    neu    pos
0     0.9413      0.000  0.503  0.497
1     -0.5719     0.258  0.644  0.099
2     0.8031      0.133  0.599  0.268
3     0.4404      0.000  0.854  0.146
4     0.9186      0.000  0.455  0.545

# Merging the sentiments back to reviews dataframe
df_c = pd.concat([df.reset_index(drop=True), d], axis=1)
df_c.head(3)
#output sample
```

	ProfileName	HelpfulnessNumerator	HelpfulnessDenominator	Score	Time	Summary	Text	compound	neg	neu	pos
JHU8GW	delmartian	1	1	5	1303862400	Good Quality Dog Food	bought several vitality canned dog food produc...	0.9413	0.000	0.503	0.497
VE5NK	dll pa	0	0	1	1346976000	Not as Advertised	product arrived labelled lumbo halted peanutst...	-0.5719	0.258	0.644	0.099
0XAIN	Natalia Corres "Natalia Corres"	1	1	4	1219017600	"Delight" says it all	connection around century light pillow city ge...	0.8031	0.133	0.599	0.268

```
# Convert scores into positive and negetive sentiments using some threshold
df_c['Sentiment'] = np.where(df_c['compound'] >= 0 , 'Positive', 'Negative')
df_c.head(5)
#output sample
```

rofileName	HelpfulnessNumerator	HelpfulnessDenominator	Score	Time	Summary	Text	compound	neg	neu	pos	Sentiment
elmartian	1	1	5	1303862400	Good Quality Dog Food	bought several vitality canned dog food produc...	0.9413	0.000	0.503	0.497	Positive
ll pa	0	0	1	1346976000	Not as Advertised	product arrived labelled lumbo halted peanutst...	-0.5719	0.258	0.644	0.099	Negative
atalia orres Natalia orres"	1	1	4	1219017600	"Delight" says it all	connection around century light pillow city ge...	0.8031	0.133	0.599	0.268	Positive

Step 2-7. Get business insights

Let's see how the overall sentiment is using the sentiment we generated.

```
result=df_c['Sentiment'].value_counts()
result.plot(kind='bar', rot=0,color='br');
```

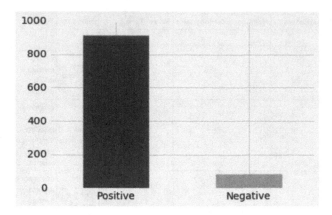

We just took a sample of 1000 reviews and completed sentiment analysis. If you look, more than 900 (>90%) reviews are positive, which is good for any business.

You can also group by-products, that is, sentiments by-products to understand the high-level customer feedback against products.

```
#Sample code snippet
result=df_c.groupby('ProductId')['Sentiment'].value_counts().unstack()
result[['Negative','Positive']].plot(kind='bar', rot=0,color='rb')
```

Similarly, you can analyze sentiments by month using the time column and many other such attributes.

Recipe 5-3. Applying Text Similarity Functions

This recipe covers data stitching using text similarity.

Problem

You have multiple tables in the database, and sometimes there won't be a common ID or KEY to join them, including in scenarios like the following.

- Customer information scattered across multiple tables and systems

- No global key to link them all together

- A lot of variations in names and addresses

Solution

This can be solved by applying text similarity functions on the demographic's columns like the first name, last name, address, and so on. And based on the similarity score on a few common columns, you can decide either the record pair is a match or not a match.

How It Works

Follow the steps in this section to link the records.

The following are the technical challenges.

- Huge records that need to be linked/stitched/deduplicated.

- Records come from various systems with differing schemas.

There is no global key or customer ID to merge. There are two possible scenarios of data stitching or linking records.

- Multiple records of the same customer at the same table, and you want to dedupe.

- Records of the same customers from multiple tables need to be merged.

For Recipe 3a, let's solve scenario 1, which is deduplication, and as a part of Recipe 3b, let's solve scenario 2, which is record linkage from multiple tables.

Deduplication in the same table

Step 3a-1. Read and understand the data

First, you need the data.

```
# Import package
!pip install recordlinkage
import recordlinkage

#For this demo let us use the built-in dataset from recordlinkage library
#import data set
from recordlinkage.datasets import import load_febrl1
```

```
#create a dataframe - dfa
dfA = load_febrl1()
dfA.head()

#output
```

	given_name	surname	street_number	address_1	address_2	suburb	postcode	state	date_of_birth	soc_sec_id
rec_id										
rec-223-org	NaN	waller	6	tullaroop street	willaroo	st james	4011	wa	19081209	6988048
rec-122-org	lachlan	berry	69	giblin street	killarney	bittern	4814	qld	19990219	7364009
rec-373-org	deakin	sondergeld	48	goldfinch circuit	kooltuo	canterbury	2776	vic	19600210	2635962
rec-10-dup-0	kayla	harrington	NaN	maltby circuit	coaling	coolaroo	3465	nsw	19150612	9004242
rec-227-org	luke	purdon	23	ramsay place	mirani	garbutt	2260	vic	19831024	8099933

Step 3a-2. Extract a blocking key

Reduce the comparison window and create record pairs.

- There is a very large number records; let's say, 100 Million records means (100 Million choose 2) $\approx 10^{16}$ possible pairs

- A heuristic is needed to quickly cut 10^{16} down without losing many matches

This can be accomplished by extracting a blocking key. The following is an example.

- Record: first name: John, last name: Roberts, address: 20 Main St Plainville MA 01111

- Blocking key: first name - John

- Paired with: John Ray ... 011

- Won't be paired with: Frank Sinatra ... 07030

- Generate pairs only for records in the same block

Here, blocking is done on the "Sndx-SN," column, which is the Soundex value of the surname column, as discussed in Chapter 4.

Database A – Blocking information

RecID	Surname	Sndx-SN	Postcode	F3D-PC
a1	smith	s530	2602	260
a2	neighan	n250	2604	260
a3	meier	m600	2050	205
a4	smithers	s536	2012	201
a5	nguyen	n250	2022	202
a6	faulkner	f425	2037	203
a7	sandy	s530	2713	271

Database B – Blocking information

RecID	Surname	Sndx-SN	Postcode	F3D-PC
b1	meier	m600	2000	200
b2	meier	m600	2604	260
b3	smith	s530	2619	261
b4	nguyen	n250	2002	200
b5	fawkner	f256	2037	203
b6	santi	s530	2113	211
b7	cain	c500	2020	202

Candidate record pairs generated from Surname blocking

BKVs	Candidate record pairs
m600	(a3, b1), (a3, b2)
n250	(a2, b4), (a5, b4)
s530	(a1, b3), (a1, b6), (a7, b3), (a7, b6)

(a1, b2)
(a1, b3)
(a1, b6)
(a2, b2)
(a2, b4)
(a3, b1)
(a3, b2)
(a5, b4)
(a5, b7)
(a6, b5)
(a7, b3)
(a7, b6)

Candidate record pairs generated from Postcode blocking

BKVs	Candidate record pairs
202	(a5, b7)
203	(a6, b5)
260	(a1, b2), (a2, b2)

There are many advanced blocking techniques, also, like the following.

- Standard blocking
  - Single column
  - Multiple columns
- Sorted neighborhood
- Q-gram: fuzzy blocking
- LSH
- Canopy clustering

This can be a new topic altogether, but for now, let's build the pairs using the first name as the blocking index.

```
indexer = recordlinkage.BlockIndex(on='given_name')
pairs = indexer.index(dfA)
print (len(pairs))
#output
2082
```

Step 3a-3. Do similarity matching and scoring

Here we compute the similarity scores on the columns like given name, surname, and address between the record pairs generated in the previous step. For columns like date of birth, suburb, and state, we use the exact match since it is important for this column to possess exact records.

We use Jaro-Winkler, but you can use any of the other similarity measures discussed in Chapter 4.

```
# This cell can take some time to compute.
compare_cl = recordlinkage.Compare()

compare_cl.string('given_name', 'given_name',method='jarowinkler',
label="given_name")
compare_cl.string('surname', 'surname', method="jarowinkler",
label="surname")
compare_cl.exact('date_of_birth', 'date_of_birth', label="date_of_birth")
compare_cl.exact('suburb', 'suburb', label="suburb")
compare_cl.exact('state', 'state', label="state")
compare_cl.string('address_1', 'address_1',method='jarowinkler',
label="address_1")
features = compare_cl.compute(pairs, dfA)
features.sample(5)

#output
```

rec_id	rec_id	given_name	surname	date_of_birth	suburb	state	address_1
rec-115-dup-0	rec-120-dup-0	1.0	0.458333	0	0	0	0.548693
rec-245-dup-0	rec-331-org	1.0	0.000000	0	0	0	0.567617
rec-455-dup-0	rec-95-dup-0	1.0	0.561905	0	0	0	0.438095
rec-462-dup-0	rec-462-org	1.0	0.961905	1	0	1	1.000000
rec-132-org	rec-30-dup-0	1.0	0.455556	0	0	0	0.571429

Here, record "rec-115-dup-0" is compared with "rec-120-dup-0." Since their first name (blocking column) matches, similarity scores are calculated on the common columns for these pairs.

Step 3a-4. Predict if records match using ECM classifier

The following is an unsupervised learning method to calculate the probability that the records match.

```
# select all the features except for given_name since its our blocking key
features1 = features[['suburb','state','surname','date_of_
birth','address_1']]
# Unsupervised learning - probabilistic
ecm = recordlinkage.ECMClassifier()
result_ecm = ecm.learn((features1).astype(int),return_type = 'series')
result_ecm
#output
rec_id rec_id
rec-122-org rec-183-dup-0 0
 rec-248-org 0
 rec-469-org 0
 rec-74-org 0
 rec-183-org 0
 rec-360-dup-0 0
 rec-248-dup-0 0
 rec-469-dup-0 0
rec-183-dup-0 rec-248-org 0
 rec-469-org 0
 rec-74-org 0
 rec-183-org 1
 rec-360-dup-0 0
 rec-248-dup-0 0
 rec-469-dup-0 0
rec-248-org rec-469-org 0
 rec-74-org 0
 rec-360-dup-0 0
```

```
 rec-469-dup-0 0
rec-122-dup-0 rec-122-org 1
 rec-183-dup-0 0
 rec-248-org 0
 rec-469-org 0
 rec-74-org 0
 rec-183-org 0
 rec-360-dup-0 0
 rec-248-dup-0 0
 rec-469-dup-0 0
rec-469-org rec-74-org 0
rec-183-org rec-248-org 0

 ..
rec-208-dup-0 rec-208-org 1
rec-363-dup-0 rec-363-org 1
rec-265-dup-0 rec-265-org 1
rec-315-dup-0 rec-315-org 1
rec-410-dup-0 rec-410-org 1
rec-290-org rec-93-org 0
rec-460-dup-0 rec-460-org 1
rec-499-dup-0 rec-499-org 1
rec-11-dup-0 rec-11-org 1
rec-97-dup-0 rec-97-org 1
rec-213-dup-0 rec-421-dup-0 0
rec-349-dup-0 rec-376-dup-0 0
rec-371-dup-0 rec-371-org 1
rec-129-dup-0 rec-129-org 1
rec-462-dup-0 rec-462-org 1
rec-328-dup-0 rec-328-org 1
rec-308-dup-0 rec-308-org 1
rec-272-org rec-308-dup-0 0
 rec-308-org 0
rec-5-dup-0 rec-5-org 1
rec-407-dup-0 rec-407-org 1
rec-367-dup-0 rec-367-org 1
```

```
rec-103-dup-0 rec-103-org 1
rec-195-dup-0 rec-195-org 1
rec-184-dup-0 rec-184-org 1
rec-252-dup-0 rec-252-org 1
rec-48-dup-0 rec-48-org 1
rec-298-dup-0 rec-298-org 1
rec-282-dup-0 rec-282-org 1
rec-327-org rec-411-org 0
```

The output clearly shows that "rec-183-dup-0" matches "rec-183-org" and can be linked to one global ID. What we have done so far is called deduplication: identifying multiple records of the same users from the individual table.

Records of same customers from multiple tables

Next, let's look at how you can solve this problem if records are in multiple tables without unique IDs to merge with.

Step 3b-1. Read and understand the data

Let's use the built-in dataset from the recordlinkage library.

```
from recordlinkage.datasets import load_febrl4
dfA, dfB = load_febrl4()
dfA.head()
```

#output

	given_name	surname	street_number	address_1	address_2	suburb	postcode	state	date_of_birth	soc_sec_id
rec_id										
rec-1070-org	michaela	neumann	8	stanley street	miami	winston hills	4223	nsw	19151111	5304218
rec-1016-org	courtney	painter	12	pinkerton circuit	bega flats	richlands	4560	vic	19161214	4066625
rec-4405-org	charles	green	38	salkauskas crescent	kela	dapto	4566	nsw	19480930	4365168
rec-1288-org	vanessa	parr	905	macquoid place	broadbridge manor	south grafton	2135	sa	19951119	9239102
rec-3585-org	mikayla	malloney	37	randwick road	avalind	hoppers crossing	4552	vic	19860208	7207688

```
dfB.head()
#output
```

	given_name	surname	street_number	address_1	address_2	suburb	postcode	state	date_of_birth	soc_sec_id
rec_id										
rec-561-dup-0	elton	NaN	3	light setreet	pinehill	windermere	3212	vic	19651013	1551941
rec-2642-dup-0	mitchell	maxon	47	edkins street	lochaoair	north ryde	3355	nsw	19390212	8859999
rec-608-dup-0	NaN	white	72	lambrigg street	kelgoola	broadbeach waters	3159	vic	19620216	9731855
rec-3239-dup-0	elk i	menzies	1	lyster place	NaN	northwood	2585	vic	19980624	4970481
rec-2886-dup-0	NaN	garanggar	NaN	may maxwell crescent	springettst arcade	forest hill	2342	vic	19921016	1366884

Step 3b-2. Block to reduce the comparison window and create record pairs

This is the same as explained previously, considering the given_name as a blocking index.

```
indexer = recordlinkage.BlockIndex(on='given_name')
pairs = indexer.index(dfA, dfB)
```

Step 3b-3. Do similarity matching

The explanation remains the same.

```
compare_cl = recordlinkage.Compare()
compare_cl.string('given_name', 'given_name',method='jarowinkler',
label="given_name")
compare_cl.string('surname', 'surname', method="jarowinkler",
label="surname")
compare_cl.exact('date_of_birth', 'date_of_birth', label="date_of_birth")
compare_cl.exact('suburb', 'suburb', label="suburb")
compare_cl.exact('state', 'state', label="state")
compare_cl.string('address_1', 'address_1',method='jarowinkler',
label="address_1")
features = compare_cl.compute(pairs, dfA, dfB)
features.head(10)
#output
```

rec_id	rec_id	given_name	surname	date_of_birth	suburb	state	address_1
	rec-3024-dup-0	1.0	0.436508	0	0	1	0.000000
	rec-2371-dup-0	1.0	0.490079	0	0	0	0.715873
rec-1070-org	rec-4652-dup-0	1.0	0.490079	0	0	0	0.645604
	rec-4795-dup-0	1.0	0.000000	0	0	1	0.552381
	rec-1314-dup-0	1.0	0.000000	0	0	1	0.618254
	rec-3024-dup-0	1.0	0.527778	0	0	0	0.000000
	rec-2371-dup-0	1.0	1.000000	1	1	1	1.000000
rec-2371-org	rec-4652-dup-0	1.0	0.500000	0	0	1	0.635684
	rec-4795-dup-0	1.0	0.527778	0	0	0	0.411111
	rec-1314-dup-0	1.0	0.527778	0	0	0	0.672222

So here record "rec-1070-org" is compared with "rec-3024-dup-0," "rec-2371-dup-0," "rec-4652-dup-0," "rec-4795-dup-0," and "rec-1314-dup-0, since their first name (blocking column) is matching and similarity scores are calculated on the common columns for these pairs.

Step 3b-4. Predict if records match using ECM classifier

The following is an unsupervised learning method to calculate the probability that the record is a match.

```
# select all the features except for given_name since its our blocking key
features1 = features[['suburb','state','surname','date_of_
birth','address_1']]
# unsupervised learning - probablistic
ecm = recordlinkage.ECMClassifier()
result_ecm = ecm.learn((features1).astype(int),return_type = 'series')
result_ecm
#output sample
rec_id          rec_id
rec-1070-org    rec-3024-dup-0     0
                rec-2371-dup-0     0
```

```
                    rec-4652-dup-0    0
                    rec-4795-dup-0    0
                    rec-1314-dup-0    0
rec-2371-org        rec-3024-dup-0    0
                    rec-2371-dup-0    1
                    rec-4652-dup-0    0
                    rec-4795-dup-0    0
                    rec-1314-dup-0    0
rec-3582-org        rec-3024-dup-0    0
                    rec-2371-dup-0    0
                    rec-4652-dup-0    0
                    rec-4795-dup-0    0
                    rec-1314-dup-0    0
rec-3024-org        rec-3024-dup-0    1
                    rec-2371-dup-0    0
                    rec-4652-dup-0    0
                    rec-4795-dup-0    0
                    rec-1314-dup-0    0
rec-4652-org        rec-3024-dup-0    0
                    rec-2371-dup-0    0
                    rec-4652-dup-0    1
                    rec-4795-dup-0    0
                    rec-1314-dup-0    0
rec-4795-org        rec-3024-dup-0    0
                    rec-2371-dup-0    0
                    rec-4652-dup-0    0
                    rec-4795-dup-0    1
                    rec-1314-dup-0    0
                                 ..
rec-2820-org        rec-2820-dup-0    1
                    rec-991-dup-0     0
rec-1984-org        rec-1984-dup-0    1
rec-1662-org        rec-1984-dup-0    0
rec-4415-org        rec-1984-dup-0    0
rec-1920-org        rec-1920-dup-0    1
```

rec-303-org	rec-303-dup-0	1
rec-1915-org	rec-1915-dup-0	1
rec-4739-org	rec-4739-dup-0	1
	rec-4865-dup-0	0
rec-681-org	rec-4276-dup-0	0
rec-4603-org	rec-4848-dup-0	0
	rec-4603-dup-0	1
rec-3122-org	rec-4848-dup-0	0
	rec-4603-dup-0	0
rec-3711-org	rec-3711-dup-0	1
rec-4912-org	rec-4912-dup-0	1
rec-664-org	rec-664-dup-0	1
	rec-1311-dup-0	0
rec-4031-org	rec-4031-dup-0	1
rec-1413-org	rec-1413-dup-0	1
rec-735-org	rec-735-dup-0	1
rec-1361-org	rec-1361-dup-0	1
rec-3090-org	rec-3090-dup-0	1
rec-2571-org	rec-2571-dup-0	1
rec-4528-org	rec-4528-dup-0	1
rec-4887-org	rec-4887-dup-0	1
rec-4350-org	rec-4350-dup-0	1
rec-4569-org	rec-4569-dup-0	1
rec-3125-org	rec-3125-dup-0	1

The output clearly shows that "rec-122-dup-0" matches "rec-122-org" and can be linked to one global ID.

In this way, you can create a data lake consisting of a unique global ID and consistent data across tables and perform statistical analysis.

Recipe 5-4. Summarizing Text Data

If you just look around, there are lots of articles and books available. Let's assume you want to learn a concept in NLP, and if you Google it, you find an article. You like the article's content, but it's too long to read it one more time. You want to summarize the article and save it somewhere so that you can read it later.

Well, NLP has a solution for that. Text summarization helps do that. You don't have to read the full article or book every time.

Problem

Text summarization of article/document using different algorithms in Python.

Solution

Text summarization is the process of making large documents into smaller ones without losing the context, which eventually saves the reader's time. This can be done using different techniques like the following.

- TextRank: A graph-based ranking algorithm

- Feature-based text summarization

- LexRank: TF-IDF with a graph-based algorithm

- Topic-based

- Using sentence embeddings

- Encoder-decoder model: Deep learning techniques

How It Works

Explore the first two approaches in this recipe.

Step 4-1. Use TextRank

TextRank is the graph-based ranking algorithm for NLP. It is inspired by PageRank, which is used in the Google search engine but particularly designed for text. It extracts the topics, creates nodes out of them, and captures the relation between nodes to summarize the text.

Let's see how to do it using Python's gensim package. The function is `summarize`.

First, let's import the notes. Let's say you're looking at a Wikipedia article on natural language processing.

```
# Import BeautifulSoup and urllib libraries to fetch data from Wikipedia.
from bs4 import BeautifulSoup
from urllib.request import urlopen

# Function to get data from Wikipedia
def get_only_text(url):
 page = urlopen(url)
 soup = BeautifulSoup(page)
 text = ' '.join(map(lambda p: p.text, soup.find_all('p')))
 print (text)
 return soup.title.text, text

# Mention the Wikipedia url
url="https://en.wikipedia.org/wiki/Natural_language_processing"
# Call the function created above
text = get_only_text(url)

# Count the number of letters
len("".join(text))
```

Result:
Out[74]: 8519
```
# Lets see first 1000 letters from the text
text[:1000]
```

Result :
Out[72]: '(\'Natural language processing - Wikipedia\', \'Natural language processing (NLP) is an area of computer science and artificial intelligence concerned with the interactions between computers and human (natural) languages, in particular how to program computers to process and analyze large amounts of natural language\\xa0data.\\n Challenges in natural language processing frequently involve speech recognition, natural language understanding, and natural language generation.\\n The history of natural language processing generally started in the 1950s, although work can be found from earlier periods.\\nIn 1950, Alan Turing published an article

titled "Intelligence" which proposed what is now called the Turing test as a criterion of intelligence.\\n The Georgetown experiment in 1954 involved fully automatic translation of more than sixty Russian sentences into English. The authors claimed that within three or five years, machine translation would be a solved problem.[2] However, real progress was '

```
# Import summarize from gensim
from gensim.summarization.summarizer import summarize
from gensim.summarization import keywords
# Convert text to string format
text = str(text)
#Summarize the text with ratio 0.1 (10% of the total words.)
summarize(text, ratio=0.1)
Result:
Out[77]: 'However, part-of-speech tagging introduced the use of hidden
Markov models to natural language processing, and increasingly, research
has focused on statistical models, which make soft, probabilistic decisions
based on attaching real-valued weights to the features making up the input
data.\nSuch models are generally more robust when given unfamiliar input,
especially input that contains errors (as is very common for real-world
data), and produce more reliable results when integrated into a larger
system comprising multiple subtasks.\\n Many of the notable early successes
occurred in the field of machine translation, due especially to work at
IBM Research, where successively more complicated statistical models were
developed.'
```

That's it. The generated summary is as simple as that. If you read this summary and the whole article, it's close enough. But still, there is a lot of room for improvement.

```
#keywords
print(keywords(text, ratio=0.1))
```

```
Result:
learning
learn
languages
process
```

systems
worlds
world
real
natural language processing
research
researched
results
result
data
statistical
hand
generation
generally
generic
general
generated
tasks
task
large
human
intelligence
input
called
calling
calls
produced
produce
produces
producing
possibly
possible
corpora
base
based

Step 4-2. Use feature-based text summarization

Your feature-based text summarization methods extract a feature from the sentence and check the importance of ranking it. Position, length, term frequency, named entity, and many other features are used to calculate the score.

Luhn's algorithm is one of the feature-based algorithms. Let's look at how to implement it using the sumy library.

```
# Install sumy
!pip install sumy
# Import the packages
from sumy.parsers.html import HtmlParser
from sumy.parsers.plaintext import PlaintextParser
from sumy.nlp.tokenizers import Tokenizer
from sumy.summarizers.lsa import LsaSummarizer
from sumy.nlp.stemmers import Stemmer
from sumy.utils import get_stop_words
from sumy.summarizers.luhn import LuhnSummarizer

# Extracting and summarizing
LANGUAGE = "english"
SENTENCES_COUNT = 10

url="https://en.wikipedia.org/wiki/Natural_language_processing"
parser = HtmlParser.from_url(url, Tokenizer(LANGUAGE))
summarizer = LsaSummarizer()
summarizer = LsaSummarizer(Stemmer(LANGUAGE))
summarizer.stop_words = get_stop_words(LANGUAGE)
for sentence in summarizer(parser.document, SENTENCES_COUNT):
    print(sentence)
Result :
[2] However, real progress was much slower, and after the ALPAC report in
1966, which found that ten-year-long research had failed to fulfill the
expectations, funding for machine translation was dramatically reduced.
However, there is an enormous amount of non-annotated data available
(including, among other things, the entire content of the World Wide Web ),
which can often make up for the inferior results if the algorithm used has
```

a low enough time complexity to be practical, which some such as Chinese Whispers do.

Since the so-called "statistical revolution"

in the late 1980s and mid 1990s, much natural language processing research has relied heavily on machine learning .

Increasingly, however, research has focused on statistical models , which make soft, probabilistic decisions based on attaching real-valued weights to each input feature.

Natural language understanding Convert chunks of text into more formal representations such as first-order logic structures that are easier for computer programs to manipulate.

[18] ^ Implementing an online help desk system based on conversational agent Authors: Alisa Kongthon, Chatchawal Sangkeettrakarn, Sarawoot Kongyoung and Choochart Haruechaiyasak.

[self-published source] ^ Chomskyan linguistics encourages the investigation of " corner cases " that stress the limits of its theoretical models (comparable to pathological phenomena in mathematics), typically created using thought experiments , rather than the systematic investigation of typical phenomena that occur in real-world data, as is the case in corpus linguistics .

^ Antonio Di Marco - Roberto Navigili, "Clustering and Diversifying Web Search Results with Graph Based Word Sense Induction" , 2013 Goldberg, Yoav (2016).

Scripts, plans, goals, and understanding: An inquiry into human knowledge structures ^ Kishorjit, N., Vidya Raj RK., Nirmal Y., and Sivaji B.

^ PASCAL Recognizing Textual Entailment Challenge (RTE-7) https://tac.nist. gov//2011/RTE/ ^ Yi, Chucai; Tian, Yingli (2012), "Assistive Text Reading from Complex Background for Blind Persons" , Camera-Based Document Analysis and Recognition , Springer Berlin Heidelberg, pp.

Problem solved. Now you don't have to read all the notes; just read the summary whenever we are running low on time.

You can use deep learning techniques to get better accuracy and better results, like the encoder-decoder model. You see how to do that in the next chapter.

Recipe 5-5. Clustering Documents

Document clustering, also called *text clustering*, is a cluster analysis of textual documents. One of the typical usages would be document management.

Problem

You want to cluster or group the documents based on patterns and similarities.

Solution

Document clustering includes similar steps.

1. Tokenization.

2. Stemming and lemmatization.

3. Removing stop words and punctuation.

4. Computing term frequencies or TF-IDF.

5. Clustering: k-means/hierarchical. You can then use any of the clustering algorithms to cluster different documents based on the features we have generated

6. Evaluation and visualization: The clustering results can be visualized by plotting the clusters into a two-dimensional space.

How It Works

Step 5-1. Import data and libraries

The following are the libraries, followed by the data.

```
!pip install mpld3
import numpy as np
import pandas as pd
import nltk
from nltk.stem.snowball import SnowballStemmer
from bs4 import BeautifulSoup
```

```
import re
import os
import codecs
from sklearn import feature_extraction
import mpld3
from sklearn.metrics.pairwise import cosine_similarity
import os
import matplotlib.pyplot as plt
import matplotlib as mpl
from sklearn.manifold import MDS

#Lets use the same complaint dataset we use for classification
Data = pd.read_csv("/Consumer_Complaints.csv",encoding='latin-1')
#selecting required columns and rows
Data = Data[['consumer_complaint_narrative']]
Data = Data[pd.notnull(Data['consumer_complaint_narrative'])]

# lets do the clustering for just 200 documents. Its easier to interpret.
Data_sample=Data.sample(200)
```

Step 5-2. Preprocess and use TF-IDF feature engineering

Now let's preprocess it.

```
# Remove unwanted symbol
Data_sample['consumer_complaint_narrative'] = Data_sample['consumer_
complaint_narrative'].str.replace('XXXX',")
# Convert dataframe to list
complaints = Data_sample['consumer_complaint_narrative'].tolist()
# create the rank of documents - we will use it later
ranks = []
for i in range(1, len(complaints)+1):
    ranks.append(i)
# Stop Words
stopwords = nltk.corpus.stopwords.words('english')
# Load 'stemmer'
stemmer = SnowballStemmer("english")
```

```python
# Functions for sentence tokenizer, to remove numeric tokens and raw
#punctuation
def tokenize_and_stem(text):
    tokens = [word for sent in nltk.sent_tokenize(text) for word in nltk.
    word_tokenize(sent)]
    filtered_tokens = []
    for token in tokens:
        if re.search('[a-zA-Z]', token):
            filtered_tokens.append(token)
    stems = [stemmer.stem(t) for t in filtered_tokens]
    return stems
def tokenize_only(text):
    tokens = [word.lower() for sent in nltk.sent_tokenize(text) for word in
    nltk.word_tokenize(sent)]
    filtered_tokens = []
    for token in tokens:
        if re.search('[a-zA-Z]', token):
            filtered_tokens.append(token)
    return filtered_tokens
from sklearn.feature_extraction.text import TfidfVectorizer
# tfidf vectorizer
tfidf_vectorizer = TfidfVectorizer(max_df=0.8, max_features=200000,
                                   min_df=0.2, stop_words="english",
                                   use_idf=True, tokenizer=tokenize_and_stem,
                                   ngram_range=(1,3))
#fit the vectorizer to data
tfidf_matrix = tfidf_vectorizer.fit_transform(complaints)
terms = tfidf_vectorizer.get_feature_names()
print(tfidf_matrix.shape)
(200, 30)
```

Step 5-3. Cluster using k-means

Let's start the clustering.

```
#Import Kmeans
from sklearn.cluster import KMeans

# Define number of clusters
num_clusters = 6

#Running clustering algorithm
km = KMeans(n_clusters=num_clusters)
km.fit(tfidf_matrix)

#final clusters
clusters = km.labels_.tolist()
complaints_data = { 'rank': ranks, 'complaints': complaints,
                'cluster': clusters }
frame = pd.DataFrame(complaints_data, index = [clusters] , columns =
['rank', 'cluster'])
#number of docs per cluster
frame['cluster'].value_counts()
```

```
0 42
1 37
5 36
3 36
2 27
4 22
```

Step 5-4. Identify cluster behavior

Identify the top five words that are nearest to the cluster centroid.

```
totalvocab_stemmed = []
totalvocab_tokenized = []
for i in complaints:
    allwords_stemmed = tokenize_and_stem(i)
    totalvocab_stemmed.extend(allwords_stemmed)
```

```
    allwords_tokenized = tokenize_only(i)
    totalvocab_tokenized.extend(allwords_tokenized)
vocab_frame = pd.DataFrame({'words': totalvocab_tokenized}, index =
totalvocab_stemmed)
#sort cluster centers by proximity to centroid
order_centroids = km.cluster_centers_.argsort()[:, ::-1]
for i in range(num_clusters):
    print("Cluster %d words:" % i, end=")
    for ind in order_centroids[i, :6]:
        print(' %s' % vocab_frame.ix[terms[ind].split(' ')].values.tolist()
        [0][0].encode('utf-8', 'ignore'), end=',')
    print()
Cluster 0 words: b'needs', b'time', b'bank', b'information', b'told'
Cluster 1 words: b'account', b'bank', b'credit', b'time', b'months'
Cluster 2 words: b'debt', b'collection', b'number', b'credit', b"n't"
Cluster 3 words: b'report', b'credit', b'credit', b'account', b'information'
Cluster 4 words: b'loan', b'payments', b'pay', b'months', b'state'
Cluster 5 words: b'payments', b'pay', b'told', b'did', b'credit'
```

Step 5-5. Plot the clusters on a 2D graph

Finally, plot the clusters.

```
#Similarity
similarity_distance = 1 - cosine_similarity(tfidf_matrix)

# Convert two components as we're plotting points in a two-dimensional plane
mds = MDS(n_components=2, dissimilarity="precomputed", random_state=1)
pos = mds.fit_transform(similarity_distance)  # shape (n_components,
     n_samples)
xs, ys = pos[:, 0], pos[:, 1]
#Set up colors per clusters using a dict
cluster_colors = {0: '#1b9e77', 1: '#d95f02', 2: '#7570b3', 3: '#e7298a',
                4: '#66a61e', 5: '#D2691E'}
#set up cluster names using a dict
```

```python
cluster_names = {0: 'property, based, assist',
                 1: 'business, card',
                 2: 'authorized, approved, believe',
                 3: 'agreement, application,business',
                 4: 'closed, applied, additional',
                 5: 'applied, card'}
# Finally plot it
%matplotlib inline

#Create data frame that has the result of the MDS and the cluster
df = pd.DataFrame(dict(x=xs, y=ys, label=clusters))
groups = df.groupby('label')
# Set up plot
fig, ax = plt.subplots(figsize=(17, 9)) # set size
for name, group in groups:
    ax.plot(group.x, group.y, marker="o", linestyle='', ms=20,
            label=cluster_names[name], color=cluster_colors[name],
            mec='none')
    ax.set_aspect('auto')
    ax.tick_params(\
        axis= 'x',
        which='both',
        bottom='off',
        top='off',
        labelbottom='off')
    ax.tick_params(\
        axis= 'y',
        which='both',
        left='off',
        top='off',
        labelleft='off')

ax.legend(numpoints=1)
plt.show()
```

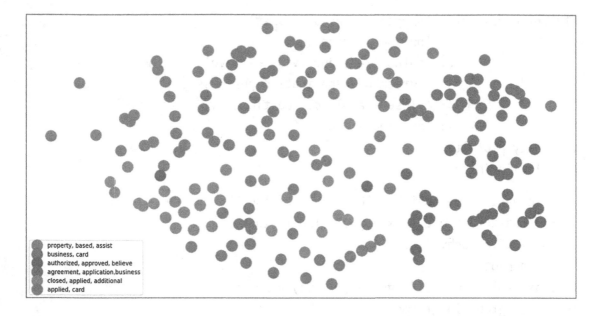

property, based, assist
business, card
authorized, approved, believe
agreement, application,business
closed, applied, additional
applied, card

That's it. There are 200 complaints clustered into six groups using k-means clustering. It clusters similar kinds of complaints into six buckets using TF-IDF. You can also use the word embeddings and solve this to achieve better clusters. 2D graphs provide an easy-to-understand look into the cluster's behavior. You see that the same color dots (docs) are located closer to each other.

Recipe 5-6. NLP in a Search Engine

This recipe discusses what it takes to build a search engine from an NLP standpoint. Implementation is beyond the scope of this book, however.

Problem

You want to know the architecture and NLP pipeline to build a search engine.

Solution

Figure 5-1 shows the whole process. Each step is explained in the "How It Works" section.

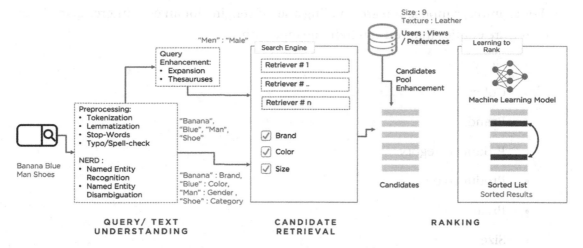

Figure 5-1. *The NLP process in a search engine*

How It Works

Follow the architecture step by step to build a search engine from an NLP standpoint.

Step 6-1. Preprocess

Whenever the user enters the search query, it is passed on to the NLP preprocessing pipeline.

1. Removal of noise and stop words

2. Tokenization

3. Stemming

4. Lemmatization

Step 6-2. Use the entity extraction model

Output from the pipeline is fed into the entity extraction model. You can build the customized entity recognition model by using any of the libraries like StanfordNER or NLTK.

Or you can build an entity recognition model from scratch using conditional random fields or Markov models.

For example, suppose you are building a search engine for an ecommerce giant. The following are entities that you can train the model on.

- Gender

- Color

- Brand

- Product category

- Product type

- Price

- Size

You can build named entity disambiguation using deep learning frameworks like RNN and LSTM. This is very important for the entities extractor to understand the content in which the entities are used. For example, pink can be a color or a brand. NED helps in such disambiguation.

NERD Model building steps.

- Data cleaning and preprocessing

- Training the NER model

- Testing and validation

- Deployment

Ways to train/build the NERD model

- Named-entity recognition and disambiguation

- Stanford NER with customization

- Recurrent neural network (RNN) – LSTM (long short-term memory) to use context for disambiguation

- Joint named-entity recognition and disambiguation

Step 6-3. Do query enhancement/expansion

It is very important to understand the possible synonyms of the entities to make sure search results do not miss out on potential relevance. For example, men's shoes can also be called *male shoes*, *men's sports shoes*, *men's formal shoes*, *men's loafers*, or *men's sneakers*.

Use locally trained word embedding (using the word2vec/**GloVe** model**) to achieve this.**

Step 6-4. Use a search platform

Search platforms such as Solr or Elasticsearch have major features that include full-text search hit highlighting, faceted search, real-time indexing, dynamic clustering, and database integration. This is not related to NLP. From an end-to-end application point of view, we have just introduced you to what this is.

Step 6-5. Learn to rank

Once the search results are fetched from Solr or Elasticsearch, they should be ranked based on the user preferences using the past behaviors.

Recipe 5-7. Detecting Fake News

In the era of social media, fake news is posing a lot of problems. Of course, no one would have imagined that fake news would be one of the biggest problems of this era. But, like all problems, data science has a solution for this problem as well, if not with great accuracy, with some acceptable accuracy.

Problem

Why is fake news an important problem to solve? The creation and spreading of fake news have increased significantly in recent years, mainly on social media platforms like WhatsApp, Facebook, and Instagram. Fake news can occur in any type of news—political, local, health, entertainment, technology-related issues, and beyond. A lot of wrong decisions have been made based on fake news that wasn't validated. It's challenging to differentiate between fake and real news.

The goal is to build a binary classification model that can differentiate between genuine news and fake news based on the content.

Solution

It's a binary classification problem. There is one class for fake news and another class for genuine news. There is a set of text documents along with the classes. The following are the steps to solve the problem.

1. First, convert the raw data to a data frame for further processing.

2. Preprocess and clean the text data.

3. After cleaning the data, feature engineering is carried out.

4. The data is explored to unearth potential insights.

5. These features build the model, in this case, a classifier model using algorithms like logistic regression, random forest, naïve Bayes, SVM, and more.

6. The hyperparameters of the model are tuned and evaluated. Finally, the results of the model are validated.

How It Works
Step 7-1. Collect data

Let's use the free source dataset at http://web.eecs.umich.edu/~mihalcea/downloads/ fakeNewsDatasets.zip/. A small portion of the data is already labeled.

The "fake news" dataset contains six different domains: business, technology, politics, education, sports, and entertainment. The legitimate news included in the dataset was collected from a variety of news websites, like ABC News, USA Today, CNN, New York Times, Fox News, Bloomberg, and so forth. The fake news included in this dataset consists of fake versions of the actual news written using Mechanical Turk.

All the raw news is aggregated and placed in *fakenews_dataset.csv*, which is used in this book.

Step 7-2. Install libraries

Let's import all the required libraries for this task.

```
# Data Manipulation
import pandas as pd
import numpy as np

# Visualization
import matplotlib.pyplot as plt
import seaborn as sns

# Plot the Figures Inline
%matplotlib inline

#NLP
import nltk
from nltk.corpus import stopwords
from nltk.stem import PorterStemmer
from textblob import Word
from sklearn.feature_extraction.text import TfidfVectorizer

#Machine Learning
from sklearn.ensemble import RandomForestClassifier
from sklearn import model_selection, preprocessing, linear_model,
naive_bayes, metrics, svm
from sklearn.model_selection import train_test_split
```

Step 7-3. Analyze the data

Let's import the dataset.

```
#importing dataset
df = pd.read_csv(' fakenews_dataset.csv')
df.shape

(980, 3)

df.sample(5)
```

	Category	News	Fake
270	Celebrity	Jake Gyllenhaal Is Not Here for Taylor Swift Q...	0
830	entmt	Rapper Wiz Khalifa sparks outrage for visit to...	0
566	edu	Harvard Law, Moving to Limit Applicant Pool, W...	1
752	biz	Ford to invest $1.2bn in Michigan plantsFord ...	0
359	Celebrity	Katharine McPhee Sets The Record Straight On H...	0

The data frame consists of 980 observations and three columns.

- **Category** is the category in which the news article belongs (i.e., celebrity, education (edu), etc.).

- **News** is the entire news content

- **Fake** is the label; a 1 means the news article is fake, and a 0 means it is real.

Step 7-4. Do exploratory data analysis

Let's analyze the data in depth.

```
df['Category'].value_counts()
```

```
Celebrity    500
biz           80
tech          80
sports        80
entmt         80
polit         80
edu           80
Name: Category, dtype: int64
```

```
#no. of news per category
sns.countplot(x='Category', data=df)
```

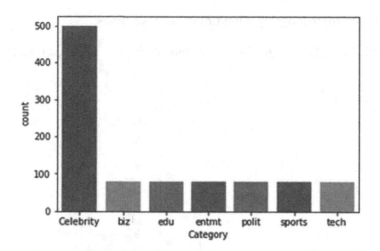

```
#adding additional column for length

df['length']=df['News'].str.len()
df.head()
```

	Category	News	Fake	length
0	Celebrity	JENNIFER ANISTON HINTS AT FRIENDS REUNIONJenni...	1	473
1	Celebrity	Brad Pitt Texts Jennifer Aniston Nonstop: Seek...	1	2349
2	Celebrity	Jennifer Aniston Pregnant With 'Miracle Baby' ...	1	2207
3	Celebrity	Heartbroken Jennifer Aniston Runs For The Bord...	1	1517
4	Celebrity	Jennifer Aniston Cheated On Brad Pitt With Mat...	1	1896

```
#Cheking max and min length of the News articles

maxlength = df['length'].max()
minlength = df['length'].min()
maxlength,minlength
```

(76490, 144)

Barplots of the article lengths of legitimate vs. fake news.

```
df.hist(column='length', by='Fake', bins=50,figsize=(12,4),color='orange')
```

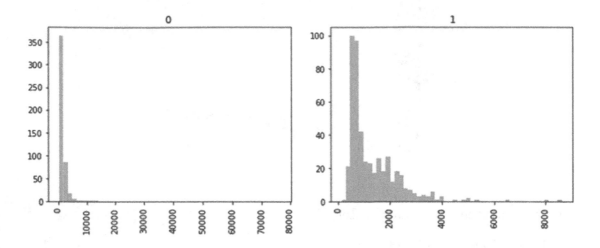

Most of the fake news articles have less than 5000 characters.

#Length of Articles with respect to the various categories.

```
df.hist(column='length', by='Category', bins=50,figsize=(20,10),color='orange')
```

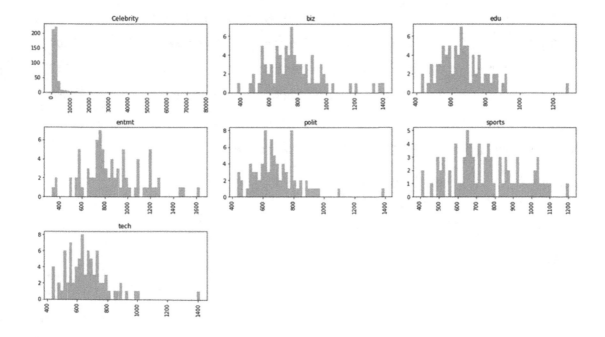

Articles about celebrities are longer than other news articles.

Step 7-5. Preprocess the data

The data preprocessing consists of the following four steps.

a. Convert **to** lowercase.

```
df['News'] = df['News'].apply(lambda x: " ".join(x.lower() for x
          in x.split()))
print(df['News'].head())
```

b. Remove punctuation.

```
df['News'] = df['News'].str.replace('[^\w\s]','')
print(df['News'].head())
```

Remove stop **words**. The stopwords are imported from the nltk library.

```
stop = stopwords.words('english')
df['News'] = df['News'].apply(lambda x: " ".join(x for x in
          x.split() if x not in stop))
```

c. Do lemmatization.

```
from nltk.stem import WordNetLemmatizer
df['News'] = df['News'].apply(lambda x: " ".join([Word(word).
          lemmatize() for word in x.split()]))
```

```
df['News'].head()
```

```
0    jennifer aniston hint friend reunionjennifer a...
1    brad pitt text jennifer aniston nonstop seek i...
2    jennifer aniston pregnant miracle baby 47 repo...
3    heartbroken jennifer aniston run border adoptj...
4    jennifer aniston cheated brad pitt matt leblan...
Name: News, dtype: object
```

Step 7-6. Use train_test_split

The train_test_split library from sklearn.model_selection is imported to split the dataframe into two parts.

```
# splitting into training and testing data
X_train,X_test,y_train,y_test=train_test_split(X,y,test_size=0.3,
random_state=100, stratify=y)
```

```
#validate the shape of train and test dataset
print (X_train.shape)
print (y_train.shape)

print (X_test.shape)
print (y_test.shape)
```

```
(686, 3)
(686,)
(294, 3)
(294,)
```

Step 7-7. Do feature engineering

The TfidfVectorizer library (from `sklearn.feature_extraction.text`) generates the features from the text.

```
tfidf_vect = TfidfVectorizer(analyzer='word', token_pattern=r'\w{1,}',
max_features=5000)
tfidf_vect.fit(df['News'])
xtrain_tfidf =  tfidf_vect.transform(X_train['News'])
xtest_tfidf =  tfidf_vect.transform(X_test['News'])
```

The features have been extracted from the text. Let's build the model as a next step.

Step 7-8. Build a model

This is a classification algorithm with fake news and real news as the classes. The text has been converted to features. Let's try various machine learning algorithms to see which one has better accuracy.

The various algorithms took into consideration to build the model.

- Naive Bayes classifier

- Linear classifier (logistics regression)

- Support Vector Machine classifier

- Random forest classifier

Let's build a generalized function that can be used for various algorithms.

```
def train_model(classifier, feature_vector_train, label, feature_vector_test):

    # fitting
    classifier.fit(feature_vector_train, label)

    # predicting
    predictions = classifier.predict(feature_vector_test)

        return metrics.accuracy_score(predictions, y_test)
```

Let's start with naive Bayes.

```
accuracy = train_model(naive_bayes.MultinomialNB(), xtrain_tfidf, y_train,
xtest_tfidf)
print ("Accuracy of Naive Bayes: ", accuracy)

Accuracy:  0.47959183673469385
```

The following is logistic regression.

```
accuracy = train_model(linear_model.LogisticRegression(), xtrain_tfidf,
y_train, xtest_tfidf)
print ("Accuracy of logistic regression: ", accuracy)

Accuracy:  0.5374149659863946
```

```
#SVM.
```

```
accuracy = train_model(svm.SVC(), xtrain_tfidf, y_train, xtest_tfidf)
print ("Accuracy of SVM: ", accuracy)

Accuracy:  0.5306122448979592
```

The following is random forest.

```
accuracy = train_model(RandomForestClassifier(), xtrain_tfidf, y_train,
xtest_tfidf)
print ("Accuracy of RandomForest: ", accuracy)
```

```
Accuracy:  0.5884353741496599
```

Observation: The binomial linear classifier (logistics regression) is considered the most suitable algorithm in this problem. Let's build the model again and understand other accuracy parameters

The `LogisticRegression()` function is present in the linear_model library in sklearn.

```
#fit the model
model=linear_model.LogisticRegression()
nb = model.fit(xtrain_tfidf,y_train)
nb
```

The classifier model's result shows the prediction in the form of a binary array, where 1 means fake and 0 means legit.

```
## Model Results:
```

```
predictions = nb.predict(xtest_tfidf)
predictions
```

```
array([0, 0, 0, 1, 1, 0, 0, 1, 0, 1, 1, 1, 1, 0, 1, 0, 1, 1, 0, 0, 1, 1,
       1, 0, 0, 1, 0, 0, 0, 1, 1, 0, 0, 1, 1, 0, 0, 1, 1, 1, 0, 1, 0, 0,
       0, 0, 1, 1, 0, 1, 0, 1, 0, 0, 0, 1, 1, 1, 0, 1, 0, 1, 1, 1, 1, 0,
       0, 0, 0, 1, 1, 1, 1, 1, 0, 1, 0, 1, 0, 1, 0, 1, 0, 0, 1, 0, 1, 1,
       0, 0, 0, 1, 1, 1, 0, 0, 1, 1, 1, 1, 1, 1, 1, 0, 1, 1, 0, 1, 0, 0,
       1, 0, 0, 1, 1, 0, 0, 1, 0, 0, 0, 1, 1, 0, 0, 0, 0, 1, 1, 1, 0, 1,
       1, 1, 1, 0, 0, 0, 0, 1, 1, 1, 1, 0, 1, 0, 0, 1, 0, 0, 0, 0, 0, 1,
       0, 0, 1, 1, 1, 0, 1, 0, 1, 1, 0, 0, 1, 1, 0, 1, 1, 0, 0, 0, 1, 0,
       1, 0, 0, 0, 0, 1, 0, 1, 0, 1, 0, 0, 0, 1, 0, 0, 0, 0, 1, 1, 1, 0,
       0, 1, 1, 0, 0, 0, 0, 1, 0, 0, 0, 1, 1, 1, 1, 0, 0, 0, 1, 1, 0, 1,
       0, 0, 1, 0, 1, 0, 0, 0, 0, 0, 1, 1, 0, 0, 0, 0, 0, 0, 1, 0, 0, 1,
       1, 1, 0, 1, 0, 1, 0, 1, 1, 0, 0, 1, 1, 1, 0, 1, 1, 1, 0, 0, 1, 0,
       1, 1, 0, 0, 1, 0, 0, 0, 1, 0, 0, 1, 1, 1, 0, 0, 1, 0, 1, 0, 0, 0,
       1, 1, 1, 0, 1, 0, 1, 0], dtype=int64)
```

Model Evaluation

The classifier model can be evaluated based on two parameters.

a.   Confusion matrix

TN	FP
FN	TP

The following is the confusion matrix report for the model.

```
from sklearn.metrics import confusion_matrix
from sklearn.metrics import classification_report
print(classification_report(y_test, predictions,
target_names=["Legit", "Fake"]))
```

	precision	recall	f1-score	support
Legit	0.54	0.56	0.55	147
Fake	0.54	0.52	0.53	147
avg / total	0.54	0.54	0.54	294

The data's total f1 score is 54%.

b.   AUC (area under curve) score

$$\text{Sensitivity} = \frac{TP}{TP + FN}$$

$$\text{Specificity} = \frac{TN}{TN + FP}$$

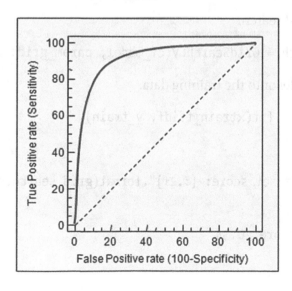

```
AUC for the built model.
from sklearn.metrics import roc_auc_score
nb_auc = roc_auc_score(y_test, nb.predict_proba(xtest_tfidf)[:, 1])
print("AUC for Model: {:.3f}".format(nb_auc))

AUC for Model: 0.559
```

The area under the curve is 56%.

You can see that there is an accuracy of up to 55%. You can increase the accuracy through more labeled data collection and tuning the parameters.

Let's see can hyperparameter tuning increase the accuracy.

Step 7-9. Tune hyperparameters

Let's use *grid search parameter* tuning, which methodically builds and evaluates a model for each combination of parameters specified in a grid.

The following are the steps for hyperparameters tuning.

1. Import the parameters grid.

   ```
   from sklearn.model_selection import GridSearchCV
   param_grid = {'C': [0.001, 0.01, 0.1, 1, 10, 15,20,100]}
   ```

2. Fit the model.

   ```
   cf_model=linear_model.LogisticRegression()
   ```

3. Run the grid search.

   ```
   grid_search = GridSearchCV(cf_model, param_grid, cv=5)
   ```

4. Fit the model onto the training data.

   ```
   grid_search.fit(xtrain_tfidf, y_train)
   ```

5. Evaluate.

   ```
   print("Test set score: {:.2f}".format(grid_search.score(xtest_tfidf,
   y_test)))

   Test set score: 0.54
   ```

6. Find the model's best parameters.

```
print("Best parameters: {}".format(grid_search.best_params_))
print("Best cross-validation score: {:.2f}".format(grid_search.
best_score_))
```

```
Best parameters: {'C': 20}
Best cross-validation score: 0.55
```

```
print("Best estimator:\n{}".format(grid_search.best_estimator_))
Best estimator:
LogisticRegression(C=20, class_weight=None, dual=False,
fit_intercept=True,
          intercept_scaling=1, max_iter=100, multi_class='ovr',
          n_jobs=1,
          penalty='l2', random_state=None, solver='liblinear',
          tol=0.0001,
          verbose=0, warm_start=False)
```

7. Rebuild the model using these tuned parameters.

```
model=linear_model.LogisticRegression(C=20, class_weight=None,
dual=False, fit_intercept=True,
          intercept_scaling=1, max_iter=100, multi_class='ovr',
          n_jobs=1,
          penalty='l2', random_state=None, solver='liblinear',
          tol=0.0001,
          verbose=0, warm_start=False)
nb=model.fit(xtrain_tfidf, y_train)
nb
```

```
LogisticRegression(C=20, class_weight=None, dual=False,
fit_intercept=True,
          intercept_scaling=1, max_iter=100, multi_class='ovr',
          n_jobs=1,
          penalty='l2', random_state=None, solver='liblinear',
          tol=0.0001,
          verbose=0, warm_start=False)
```

Step 7-10. Validate

Once the model has been fitted with the best parameters, it is cross-validated to check the model's accuracy on the text data. The validation parameters are the same.

   The following is the confusion matrix report for the model.

```
from sklearn.metrics import confusion_matrix
from sklearn.metrics import classification_report

print(classification_report(y_test, predictions,target_names=["Legit", "Fake"]))
```

```
                precision    recall  f1-score   support

       Legit         0.53      0.54      0.53       147
        Fake         0.53      0.52      0.53       147

    accuracy                            0.53       294
   macro avg         0.53      0.53      0.53       294
weighted avg         0.53      0.53      0.53       294
```

```
AUC for the tuned model.
from sklearn.metrics import roc_auc_score
nb_auc = roc_auc_score(y_test, nb.predict_proba(xtest_tfidf)[:, 1])
print("AUC for tuned SVC model: {:.3f}".format(nb_auc))
```

```
AUC for tuned SVC model: 0.525
```

Summary

This recipe built a baseline model for fake news classification and used a free source labeled dataset from multiple news channel sources. First, you learned how to create the dataset, preprocess the data, and perform feature engineering using TF-IDF. Later you saw different machine learning methods to train the model. Finally, you observed that a linear classifier performed better when compared to other classifiers.

   There is a lot of room for increasing the accuracy using different approaches. This is just the baseline model, and you can improve the accuracy using advanced feature engineering techniques like word embeddings. You can also use deep learning methods to investigate if there are any accuracy improvements.

Recipe 5-8. Movie Genre Tagging

Multi-tag/label categorization stems from the search for text categorization issues, each of which can belong to multiple predefined themes at the same time. For example, this can find the genre types to which a movie belongs based on a summary of its drawing. In a multilabel classification, a learning set consists of instances associated with a set of tags. The task is to predict an invisible instance tag set by analyzing a learning instance with a known set of tags.

Multicategory classification assumes that each sample is assigned to one and only one label: the customer can be churn or not, but not both. And for example, a multilabel classification might be that text may deal with religion, politics, finance, education, or any of these things simultaneously.

Problem

Categorizing movies into genres is one of the classic AI problems. Online movie booking platforms and review websites like IMDb tag movies into respective genres. A genre can be action, adventure, comedy, romance, and so on.

On IMDb, every movie has a genre associated with it. But the challenge is that a single movie can also have multiple genres. For example, Avengers: *Endgame* is tagged to the action, adventure, and fantasy genres.

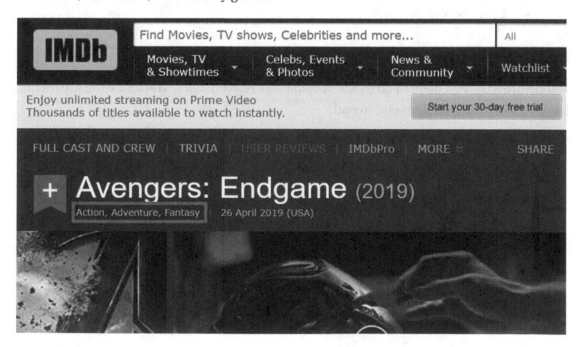

Our goal here is to tag movie genres, given the description of the movie. The model must predict all possible classes (genres) a movie could belong to. Although you have seen simple multiclass classification before, this recipe explores how to solve a multilabel learning and classification problem.

Solution

You have encountered many classification problems, and all of them were either binary class or multiclass problems. Now let's explore a unique type of problem known as *multilabel* learning to solve movie genre tagging.

So, what is multilabel classification or commonly called multilabel learning? The scenario where each observation (x) in the dataset has a target variable (y) with multiple categories. For example, movie name with description is your independent feature and the genre (action, adventure, fantasy) associated is the dependent variable.

The following are some ways to tackle multilabel problems.

- One vs. the rest

- Binary correlation

- Classification chain

- Label powerset

Approach Flow

But before that, you need to take care of usual text-related tasks. The following are the steps to solve this problem end to end.

1. Data preprocessing and cleaning

2. Feature generation

3. Exploratory data analysis

4. Multilabel classifier

5. Validation and prediction

How It Works

Step 8-1. Collect data

We are using a free source dataset that is already labeled. However, only a small portion of the data is labeled. The larger the amount of data, the greater the model's accuracy and generalization power.

Download the dataset from www.kaggle.com/cryptexcode/mpst-movie-plot-synopses-with-tags#mpst_full_data.csv.

Step 8-2. Install libraries

Import all the basic libraries required for text mining tasks.

```
# Data Manipulation
import numpy as np
import pandas as pd

# Visualization
import matplotlib.pyplot as plt
import seaborn as sns

# Plot the Figures Inline
%matplotlib inline

#Natural language processing
import nltk
from nltk.corpus import stopwords
from nltk.stem import PorterStemmer
from textblob import Word
from sklearn.feature_extraction.text import TfidfVectorizer

#Machine Learning
from sklearn.model_selection import train_test_split
```

Step 8-3. Analyze the data

Import the dataset that was downloaded earlier.

```
#Importing dataset
df = pd.read_csv('movies_genres1.csv',encoding = 'ISO-8859-1')
df.shape
```

```
(9502, 30)
```

```
#Top 5 rows to see the data
df.head()
```

	title	plot	Action	Adult	Adventure	Animation	Biography	Comedy	Crime	Documentary	...	Reality-TV	Romance	Sci-Fi	Short
0	DaysLater (2013)	#7dayslater is an interactive comedy series f...	0	0	0	0	0	1	0	0	...	0	0	0	0
1	LawstinWoods (2013) {The Happening (#1.3)}	The gang discuss their shock over realizing t...	0	0	0	0	0	0	0	0	...	0	0	1	0
2	mykpop (2013) {(#1.4)}	K-pop is growing! Check out Mnet America's ne...	0	0	0	0	0	0	0	0	...	1	0	0	0
3	Allo 'Allo! (1982) {The Generals' Conference (...	The generals gather for the conference but th...	0	0	0	0	0	1	0	0	...	0	0	0	0
4	'Til Death (2006) {Mixed Doubles (#2.5)}	Steph introduces Eddie to yoga. Jeff turns Jo...	0	0	0	0	0	1	0	0	...	0	1	0	0

```
df.columns
```

```
Index(['title', 'plot', 'Action', 'Adult', 'Adventure', 'Animation',
       'Biography', 'Comedy', 'Crime', 'Documentary', 'Drama', 'Family',
       'Fantasy', 'Game-Show', 'History', 'Horror', 'Music', 'Musical',
       'Mystery', 'News', 'Reality-TV', 'Romance', 'Sci-Fi', 'Short', 'Sport',
       'Talk-Show', 'Thriller', 'War', 'Western', 'count', 'length', 'desc'],
      dtype='object')
```

Step 8-4. Do exploratory data analysis

Concatenate the movie title and plot.

```
df["desc"] = df["title"].map(str) + df["plot"]
df = df[df['desc'].notnull()]
```

The following are the tags by genre.

```
print (df.apply(pd.to_numeric, errors='coerce').sum())
```

```
title              0.0
plot               0.0
Action           659.0
Adult              7.0
Adventure        547.0
Animation        689.0
Biography         71.0
Comedy          2217.0
Crime            914.0
Documentary     1377.0
Drama           3150.0
Family          1075.0
Fantasy          377.0
Game-Show        103.0
History          166.0
Horror           146.0
Music            194.0
Musical           29.0
Mystery          633.0
News            1069.0
Reality-TV      1008.0
Romance         1338.0
Sci-Fi           477.0
Short             61.0
Sport            286.0
Talk-Show        733.0
Thriller         488.0
```

```
War                   67.0
Western              201.0
count              18082.0
length           3623621.0
desc                   0.0
Total_tags         18082.0
dtype: float64
```

Most of the movies are tagged under drama, followed by comedy.

```
df.groupby(['Total_tags']).size()
```

```
Total_tags
1        4540
2        2969
3        1038
4         510
5         279
6         121
7          27
8          15
10          2
dtype: int64
```

4540 movies were tagged to only one genre, and about 1000 movies belong to three genres.

Step 8-5. Preprocess the data

The data preprocessing consists of the following four steps.

1. Convert **to** lowercase.

    ```
    df['desc'] = df['desc'].apply(lambda x:" ".join(x.lower() for x in
            x.split()))
    ```

2. Remove punctuation.

    ```
    df['desc'] = df['desc'].str.replace('\d+', '')
    df['desc'] = df['desc'].str.replace('[^\w\s]','')
    ```

3. Remove stop **words**.

   The stopwords are imported from the nltk library.

   ```
   stop = stopwords.words('english')
   df['desc'] = df['desc'].apply(lambda x: " ".join(x for x in
               x.split() if x not in stop))
   ```

4. **Lemmatization**.

   ```
   from nltk.stem import WordNetLemmatizer
   df['desc'] = df['desc'].apply(lambda x: " ".join([Word(word).
               lemmatize() for word in x.split()]))
   ```

   ```
   df['desc'].head()
   ```

   ```
   0    dayslater dayslater interactive comedy series ...
   1    lawstinwoods happening gang discus shock reali...
   2    mykpop kpop growing check mnet america newest ...
   3    allo allo general conference general gather co...
   4    til death mixed double steph introduces eddie ...
   Name: desc, dtype: object
   ```

The text is clean after doing the preprocessing steps and ready to move to the next steps.

Step 8-6. Use train_test_split

```
#create input dataset without including target variable( class column)
X = df['desc']
X.shape
```

```
(9501,)
```

```
#Create the target data with only class column
y = df.iloc[:,2:29]
y.shape
```

```
(9501, 27)
```

```
# splitting into training and testing data
```

```
X_train,X_test,y_train,y_test=train_test_split(X,y,test_size=0.3,
random_state=100, stratify=y)

#validate the shape of train and test dataset
print (X_train.shape)
print (y_train.shape)

print (X_test.shape)
print (y_test.shape)

(6650,)
(6650, 27)
(2851,)
(2851, 27)
```

Step 8-7. Do feature engineering

The TfidfVectorizer library (from `sklearn.feature_extraction.text`) generates the features from the text.

```
#Generating features using tfidf

tfidf_vect = TfidfVectorizer(analyzer='word', token_pattern=r'\w{1,}',
max_features=5000)
tfidf_vect.fit(df['desc'])

xtrain_tfidf =  tfidf_vect.transform(X_train)
xtest_tfidf =  tfidf_vect.transform(X_test)
```

Step 8-8. Do model building and prediction

There are two ways this problem can be solved. Let's look at all the approaches and implement them using different libraries.

- Problem transformation

- Algorithm adaptation

Let's start with problem transformation methods.

Problem Transformation

The basic idea behind problem transformation methods is converting the multilabel into a single label using data manipulation techniques. This is done using skmultilearn package, which enables different kinds of transformations.

There are three types of transformations possible. Let's discuss all three and implement them using the following libraries: binary relevance,

Binary Relevance

Binary relevance converts each label into a different single class classification problem. If you have five labels, this approach creates five new datasets for one label. These created datasets are used for single-label classifiers separately.

x	y
text1	y1, y2
text2	y2,y3
text3	y1, y2
text4	y1,y3

x	y1
text1	1
text2	0
text3	1
text4	1

x	y2
text1	1
text2	1
text3	1
text4	0

x	y3
text1	0
text2	1
text3	0
text4	1

Let's implement the method and see what the results look like.

```
# Import the packages

from skmultilearn.problem_transform import BinaryRelevance
from sklearn.naive_bayes import GaussianNB
```

```
# initialize binary relevance multi-label classifier with a gaussian naive
Bayes base classifier

classifier = BinaryRelevance(GaussianNB())

# train the algorithms
classifier.fit(xtrain_tfidf, y_train)

# predict
predictions = classifier.predict(xtest_tfidf)

#output
print(predictions)
(16, 0)         1
  (38, 0)       1
  (42, 0)       1
  (49, 0)       1
  (52, 0)       1
  (56, 0)       1
  (62, 0)       1
  (72, 0)       1
  (141, 0)      1
  (171, 0)      1
  (173, 0)      1
  (198, 0)      1
  (243, 0)      1
  (258, 0)      1
  (292, 0)      1
  (343, 0)      1
  (371, 0)      1
  (398, 0)      1
  (429, 0)      1

#Evaluation

from sklearn.metrics import accuracy_score
accuracy_score(y_test,predictions)
```

0.21220624342336022

```
metrics.hamming_loss(y_test, predictions)
```

0.07472361874326097

Please note that we are getting very bad accuracy, which is 21%. It would increase with more training data, however. You can try a few more algorithms to see if you can reach a better number.

Now let's try SVM with binary relevance, and see its performance to classify multilabel.

```
#import the library
from skmultilearn.problem_transform import BinaryRelevance
from sklearn.svm import SVC

# define the classifier

classifier = BinaryRelevance(
    classifier=SVC(),
    require_dense=[False, True]
)

# train
classifier.fit(xtrain_tfidf, y_train)

# predict
predictions = classifier.predict(xtest_tfidf)

# evaluation
accuracy_score(y_test,predictions)
```

0.09

Even SVM is not able to produce good results.

Let's move on to next type of algorithm for multilabel called *classifier* chains and see if it can increase the accuracy.

Classifier Chains

Classifier chains are a chain of classifiers and hence the name. The first classifier is between x (independent feature) and one of the labels. For the next classifiers, even the labels from previous classifiers are used as input. Let's understand this with the below example.

Here, x is the independent feature (text) and y is the label/target.

x	y
text1	y1, y2
text2	y2,y3
text3	y1, y2
text4	y1,y3

x	y1
text1	1
text2	0
text3	1
text4	1

x	y1	y2
text1	1	1
text2	0	1
text3	1	1
text4	1	0

x	y1	y2	y3
text1	1	1	0
text2	0	1	1
text3	1	1	0
text4	1	0	1

Let's implement using the multilearn library.

```
# using classifier chains
from skmultilearn.problem_transform import ClassifierChain
from sklearn.naive_bayes import GaussianNB

# initialize classifier chains multi-label classifier
# with a gaussian naive Bayes base classifier

classifier = ClassifierChain(GaussianNB())

# train
classifier.fit(xtrain_tfidf, y_train)

# predict
predictions = classifier.predict(xtest_tfidf)

accuracy_score(y_test,predictions)

0.21255699754472115
```

Even this method is not giving promising results. Let's move on to next type and see how that algorithm performs.

Label Powerset

This method converts a multilabel classifier into a multiclass classifier. A single label is created on all unique label combinations.

Let's look at it using the following example.

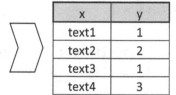

x	y
text1	y1, y2
text2	y2,y3
text3	y1, y2
text4	y1,y3

x	y
text1	1
text2	2
text3	1
text4	3

This is the implementation.

```
# using Label Powerset

from skmultilearn.problem_transform import LabelPowerset
from sklearn.naive_bayes import GaussianNB
```

```
# initialize Label Powerset multi-label classifier
# with a gaussian naive bayes base classifier

classifier = LabelPowerset(GaussianNB())

# train

classifier.fit(xtrain_tfidf, y_train)

# predict

predictions = classifier.predict(xtest_tfidf)
accuracy_score(y_test,predictions)

0.32620133286566116
```

There is a slight increase in accuracy when compared to previous methods. Let's try hyperparameter tuning to see if you can make it better.

As you know, hyperparameter tuning is one of the important aspects in improving the accuracy and choosing the best parameters for algorithms. You can leverage GridSearchCV for hyperparameters tuning, as follows.

```
#Import libraries
from skmultilearn.problem_transform import LabelPowerset
from sklearn.model_selection import GridSearchCV
from sklearn.naive_bayes import MultinomialNB
from sklearn.ensemble import RandomForestClassifier

#define the parameters

parameters = [
    {
        'classifier': [MultinomialNB()],
        'classifier__alpha': [0.7, 1.0],
    },
    {
        'classifier': [RandomForestClassifier()],
        'classifier__criterion': ['gini', 'entropy'],
        'classifier__n_estimators': [10, 20, 50],
    },
]
```

```
# tuning
clf = GridSearchCV(LabelPowerset(), parameters, scoring='accuracy')
clf.fit(xtrain_tfidf, y_train)

#print the best accuracy
print (clf.best_params_, clf.best_score_)
{'classifier': RandomForestClassifier(bootstrap=True,
class_weight=None, criterion='gini',
            max_depth=None, max_features='auto', max_leaf_nodes=None,
            min_impurity_decrease=0.0, min_impurity_split=None,
            min_samples_leaf=1, min_samples_split=2,
            min_weight_fraction_leaf=0.0, n_estimators=50,
            n_jobs=None,
            oob_score=False, random_state=None, verbose=0,
            warm_start=False), 'classifier__criterion':
'gini', 'classifier__n_estimators': 50}

0.4548872180451128
```

This is a very high improvement over the previous methods. Through tuning, you can achieve 45% accuracy.

Adapted Algorithm

An *adapted* algorithm adapts the machine learning algorithms to directly perform multilabel learning. For example, a multilabel version of kNN is represented by MLkNN.

Let's do the implementation.

```
#convert the data to matrix
y_train = y_train.as_matrix()

#import the package
from skmultilearn.adapt import MLkNN
classifier = MLkNN(k=20)

# train
classifier.fit(xtrain_tfidf, y_train)

# predict
```

```
predictions = classifier.predict(xtest_tfidf)
```

```
accuracy_score(y_test,predictions)
```

0.364784286215363

```
# import
from skmultilearn.adapt import BRkNNaClassifier
classifier = BRkNNaClassifier(k=3)
```

```
# train
classifier.fit(xtrain_tfidf, y_train)
```

```
# predict
predictions = classifier.predict(xtest_tfidf)
print(predictions)
```

```
(0, 7)        1
  (1, 5)      1
  (1, 8)      1
  (2, 8)      1
  (2, 19)     1
  (3, 17)     1
  (3, 23)     1
  (4, 23)     1
  (5, 5)      1
  (5, 9)      1
  (6, 5)      1
  (6, 20)     1
  (9, 19)     1
  (10, 7)     1
  (11, 17)    1
  (11, 23)    1
  (12, 8)     1
  (13, 2)     1
  (13, 7)     1
  (14, 8)     1
  (14, 19)    1
```

```
(15, 5)        1
(15, 9)        1
(16, 5)        1
(18, 6)        1
```

```
accuracy_score(y_test,predictions)
```

```
0.45001753770606806
```

Similarly, you can leverage support vector machine, as follows.

```
from skmultilearn.adapt import MLTSVM
classifier = MLTSVM(c_k = 2**-1)
```

```
# train
classifier.fit(xtrain_tfidf, y_train)
```

```
# predict
predictions = classifier.predict(xtest_tfidf)
```

```
accuracy_score(y_test,predictions)
```

You **have** implemented a **few end-to-end projects**. Isn't **it exciting?**

The **next chapter** looks **at** solving **problems using NLP** and deep learning.

Deep Learning for NLP

In this chapter, you implement deep learning for NLP. The following recipes are covered.

- Recipe 1. Information retrieval using deep learning

- Recipe 2. Text classification using CNN, RNN, LSTM

- Recipe 3. Predicting the next word/sequence of words using LSTM for email

- Recipe 4. Stack Overflow question recommendation

Introduction to Deep Learning

Deep learning is a subfield of machine learning that is inspired by brain functions. Just as neurons are interconnected in the brain, neural networks work the same way. Each neuron takes input, does some manipulation within the neuron, and produces output that is closer to the expected output (in the case of labeled data).

What happens within the neuron is what we are interested in to get the most accurate results. It gives weight to every input and generates a function to accumulate all these weights and pass them to the next layer, which is eventually the output layer.

The network has three components.

- Input layer

- Hidden layer/layers

- Output layer

© Akshay Kulkarni and Adarsha Shivananda 2021
A. Kulkarni and A. Shivananda, *Natural Language Processing Recipes*,
https://doi.org/10.1007/978-1-4842-7351-7_6

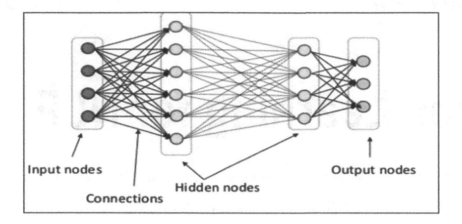

The functions can be of different types based on the problem or the data. These are also called *activation functions*. The following describes the types.

- Linear activation functions: A linear neuron takes a linear combination of the weighted input, and the output can take any value between negative infinity to infinity.

- Nonlinear activation function: These are the most used ones, and they make the output restricted between some range.

  - The sigmoid or logit activation function scales down the output between 0 and 1 by applying a log function, making the classification problems easier.

  - The softmax function is similar to sigmoid, but it calculates the probabilities of the event over n different classes, which helps determine the target in multiclass classification problems.

  - The tanh function is –1 to 1; otherwise, it is the same as sigmoid.

  - The rectified linear unit activation function converts anything that is less than zero to zero. So, the range becomes 0 to infinity.

We still haven't discussed how training is carried out in neural networks. Let's do that using the convolutional neural network.

Convolutional Neural Networks

A convolutional neural network (CNN) is similar to an ordinary neural network but has multiple hidden layers, and a filter called the *convolution layer*. CNN successfully identifies faces, objects, and traffic signs and is also used in self-driving cars.

Data

Algorithms work basically on numerical data. Images and text data are unstructured data, and they need to be converted into numerical values even before we start anything.

- *Image*: The computer takes an image as an array of pixel values. Depending on the resolution and size of the image, it sees an X * Y * Z array of numbers. For example, there is a color image, and its size is 480×480 pixels. The representation of the array is 480×480×3, where 3 is the RGB value of the color. Each of these numbers varies from 0 to 255, which describes the pixel intensity/density at that point. The concept is that if given the computer and this array of numbers, it output the probability of the image being a certain class in case of a classification problem.

- *Text*: We already discussed how to create features out of text. You can use any of those techniques to convert text to features. RNN and LSTM are better suited for text-related solutions that we discuss in the next sections.

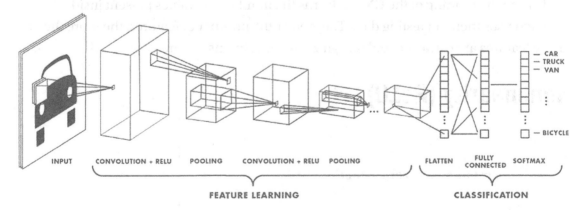

215

Architecture

CNN is a special case of a neural network with an input layer, output layer, and multiple hidden layers. The hidden layers have four different procedures to complete the network. Each one is explained in detail.

Convolution

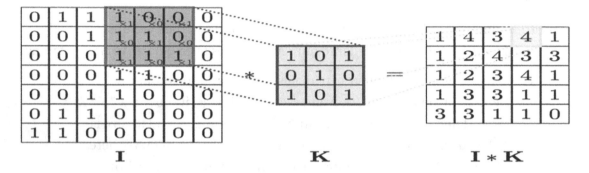

$$I \qquad K \qquad I * K$$

The convolution layer is the heart of a convolutional neural network, which does most of the computational operations. The name comes from the "convolution" operator that extracts features from the input image. These are also called *filters* (an orange 3*3 matrix). The matrix formed by sliding the filter over the full image and calculating the dot product between these two matrices is called the *convolved feature, activation map,* or the *feature map.* For example, suppose that different types of features are calculated in table data, such as "age" from "date of birth." Straight edges, simple colors, and curves are some of the features that the filter can extract from an image.

During the training of the CNN, it learns the numbers or values present inside the filter and uses them on testing data. The greater the number of features, the more the image features are extracted and recognize patterns in unseen images.

Nonlinearity (ReLU)

Output = Max(zero, Input)

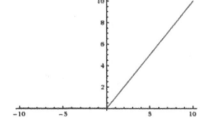

A *rectified linear unit* (**ReLU**) is a nonlinear function used after a convolution layer in CNN architecture. It replaces all negative values in the matrix with zero. The purpose of ReLU is to introduce nonlinearity in the CNN to perform better.

Pooling

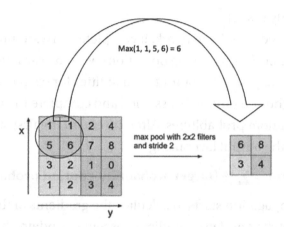

Pooling or subsampling decreases the dimensionality of the feature without losing important information. It's done to reduce the huge number of inputs to a fully connected layer and computation required to process the model. It also reduces the overfitting of the model. It uses a 2×2 window, slides over the image, and takes the maximum value in each region, as shown in the figure. This is how it reduces dimensionality.

Flatten, Fully Connected, and Softmax Layers

The last layer is a dense layer that needs feature vectors as input. But the output from the pooling layer is not a 1D feature vector. This process of converting the convolution output to a feature vector is called *flattening*. The fully connected layer takes an input from the flatten layer and gives out an *n*-dimensional vector where *n* is the number of classes. The function of the fully connected layer is to use these features for classifying the input image into various classes based on the loss function on the training dataset. The softmax function is used at the very end to convert these *n*-dimensional vectors into a probability for each class, which eventually classifies the image into a particular class.

Backpropagation: Training the Neural Network

In normal neural networks, you do forward propagation to get the output and check if this output is correct and calculate the error. In backward propagation, you go backward through your network to find the partial derivatives of the error with respect to each weight.

Let's see how exactly it works.

The input image is fed into the network. It completes forward propagation, which is convolution, ReLU, and pooling operations with forward propagation in the fully connected layer, and generates output probabilities for each class. As per the feedforward rule, weights are randomly assigned and complete the first iteration of training and output random probabilities. After the end of the first step, the network calculates the error at the output layer using

$$\textbf{Total Error} = \sum \tfrac{1}{2} \, \textbf{(target probability – output probability)}^2$$

Now, your backpropagation starts to calculate the gradients of the error with respect to all weights in the network and uses gradient descent to update all filter values and weights, which eventually minimizes the output error. Parameters like the number of filters, filter sizes, and the network architecture are finalized while building your network. The filter matrix and connection weights get updated for each run. The whole process is repeated for the complete training set until the error is minimized.

Recurrent Neural Networks

CNNs are used for computer vision problems but fail to solve sequence models. Sequence models are those where even a sequence of the entity also matters. For example, in the text, the order of the words matters to create meaningful sentences. This is where RNNs come into the picture and are useful with sequential data because each neuron can use its memory to remember information about the previous step.

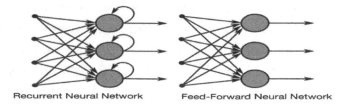

Recurrent Neural Network   Feed-Forward Neural Network

It is quite complex to understand how exactly RNN is working. If you see the above figure, recurrent neural network takes the output from the hidden layer and sends it back to the same layer before giving the prediction.

Training RNN: Backpropagation Through Time (BPTT)

You know how feedforward and backpropagation work in CNN, so let's look at how training is done in RNN.

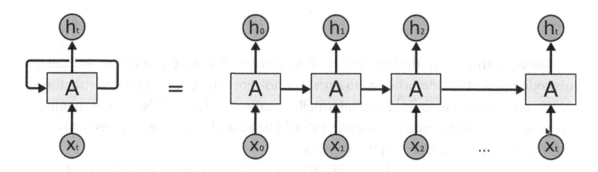

If we only discuss the hidden layer, it's not only taking input from the hidden layer, but you can also add another input to the same hidden layer. Now the backpropagation happens like any other previous training you have seen; now, it is dependent on time. Here error is backpropagated from the last timestamp to the first through unrolling the hidden layers. This allows calculating the error for each timestamp and updating the weights. Recurrent networks with recurrent connections between hidden units read an entire sequence and then produce the required output.

When the gradient values are too small, and the model takes too long to learn, this is called *vanishing gradients*. LSTM solves this problem.

Long Short-Term Memory (LSTM)

LSTMs are like RNNs but with a better equation and backpropagation, which makes them perform better. LSTMs work similarly to RNNs, but they can learn things with very long time gaps, and they can store information just like computers.

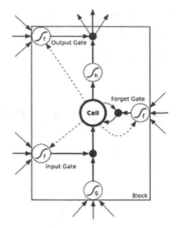

The algorithm learns the importance of the word or character through the weighing methodology and decides whether to store it or not. For this, it uses regulated structures called *gates* that can remove or add information to the cell. These cells have a sigmoid layer that decides how much information should be passed. It has three layers—input, forget, and output—to carry out this process.

An in-depth discussion of CNN and RNN work is beyond the scope of this book. There are references at the end of the book if you are interested in learning more.

Recipe 6-1. Retrieving Information

Information retrieval is one of the highly used applications of NLP, and it is quite tricky. The meaning of the words or sentences depends on the exact words used and the context and meaning. Two sentences may be of completely different words but can convey the same meaning. You should be able to capture that.

An information retrieval (IR) system allows users to efficiently search documents and retrieve meaningful information based on a search text/query.

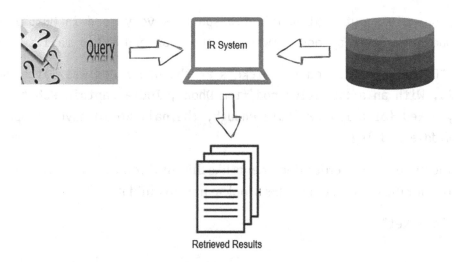

Retrieved Results

Problem

Information retrieval using word embeddings.

Solution

There are multiple ways to do information retrieval. Using word embeddings is very effective since it takes context also into consideration. We discussed how word embeddings are built in Chapter 3. The pre-trained word2vec is only used in this case.

Let's take a simple example and see how to build a document retrieval using query input. Let's say there are four documents in the database, as follows. (This showcases how it works. There are many documents in a real-world application.)

Doc1 = ["With the Union cabinet approving the amendments to the Motor Vehicles Act, 2016, those caught for drunken driving will have to have really deep pockets, as the fine payable in court has been enhanced to Rs 10,000 for first-time offenders."]

Doc2 = ["Natural language processing (NLP) is an area of computer science and artificial intelligence concerned with the interactions between computers and human (natural) languages, in particular how to program computers to process and analyze large amounts of natural language data."]

Doc3 = ["He points out that public transport is very good in Mumbai and New Delhi, where there is a good network of suburban and metro rail systems."]

Doc4 = ["But the man behind the wickets at the other end was watching just as keenly. With an affirmative nod from Dhoni, India captain Rohit Sharma promptly asked for a review. Sure enough, the ball would have clipped the top of middle and leg."]

Assume there are numerous documents like this. And you want to retrieve the most relevant one for the query "cricket." Let's look at how to build it.

```
query = "cricket"
```

How It Works

Step 1-1. Import the libraries

Here are the libraries.

```
import gensim
from gensim.models import Word2Vec
import numpy as np
import nltk
import itertools
from nltk.corpus import stopwords
from nltk.tokenize import sent_tokenize, word_tokenize
import scipy
from scipy import spatial
from nltk.tokenize.toktok import ToktokTokenizer
import re
tokenizer = ToktokTokenizer()
stopword_list = nltk.corpus.stopwords.words('english')
```

Step 1-2. Create or import documents

Randomly taking sentences from the Internet.

Doc1 = ["With the Union cabinet approving the amendments to the Motor Vehicles Act, 2016, those caught for drunken driving will have to have really deep pockets, as the fine payable in court has been enhanced to Rs 10,000 for first-time offenders."]

Doc2 = ["Natural language processing (NLP) is an area of computer science and artificial intelligence concerned with the interactions between computers and human (natural) languages, in particular how to program computers to process and analyze large amounts of natural language data."]

Doc3 = ["He points out that public transport is very good in Mumbai and New Delhi, where there is a good network of suburban and metro rail systems."]

Doc4 = ["But the man behind the wickets at the other end was watching just as keenly. With an affirmative nod from Dhoni, India captain Rohit Sharma promptly asked for a review. Sure enough, the ball would have clipped the top of middle and leg."]

```
# Put all the documents in one list

fin= Doc1+Doc2+Doc3+Doc4
```

Step 1-3. Download word2vec

Next, let's use word embeddings to solve this problem. Download word2vec from https://drive.google.com/file/d/0B7XkCwpI5KDYNlNUTTlSS21pQmM/edit.

```
#load the model

Model= gensim.models.KeyedVectors.load_word2vec_format(
'/GoogleNews-vectors-negative300.bin', binary=True)
```

Step 1-4. Create an IR system

Now, build the information retrieval system.

```
#Preprocessing

def remove_stopwords(text, is_lower_case=False):
    pattern = r'[^a-zA-z0-9\s]'
    text = re.sub(pattern, ", ".join(text))
```

```
    tokens = tokenizer.tokenize(text)
    tokens = [token.strip() for token in tokens]
    if is_lower_case:
        filtered_tokens = [token for token in tokens if token not in
                            stopword_list]
    else:
        filtered_tokens = [token for token in tokens if token.lower() not
                            in stopword_list]
    filtered_text = ' '.join(filtered_tokens)
    return filtered_text
```

```
# Function to get the embedding vector for n dimension, we have used "300"
```

```
def get_embedding(word):
    if word in model.wv.vocab:
        return model[x]
    else:
        return np.zeros(300)
```

For every document, we get a lot of vectors based on the number of words present. You need to calculate the average vector for the document through taking a mean of all the word vectors.

```
# Getting average vector for each document
out_dict =  {}
for sen in fin:
    average_vector = (np.mean(np.array([get_embedding(x) for x in
    nltk.word_tokenize(remove_stopwords(sen))]), axis=0))
    dict = { sen : (average_vector) }
    out_dict.update(dict)
```

```
# Function to calculate the similarity between the query vector and
document vector
```

```
def get_sim(query_embedding, average_vector_doc):
    sim = [(1 - scipy.spatial.distance.cosine(query_embedding,
    average_vector_doc))]
    return sim
```

```
# Rank all the documents based on the similarity to get relevant docs

def Ranked_documents(query):
    query_words =  (np.mean(np.array([get_embedding(x) for x in
                        nltk.word_tokenize(query.lower())],dtype=float), axis=0))
    rank = []
    for k,v in out_dict.items():
        rank.append((k, get_sim(query_words, v)))
    rank = sorted(rank,key=lambda t: t[1], reverse=True)
    print('Ranked Documents :')
    return rank
```

Step 1-5. Results and applications

Let's look at the information retrieval system we built works in a couple of examples.

```
# Call the IR function with a query

Ranked_documents("cricket")

Result :

[('But the man behind the wickets at the other end was watching just as
keenly. With an affirmative nod from Dhoni, India captain Rohit Sharma
promptly asked for a review. Sure enough, the ball would have clipped the
top of middle and leg.',
  [0.44954327116871795]),
 ('He points out that public transport is very good in Mumbai and
New Delhi, where there is a good network of suburban and metro rail
systems.',
  [0.23973446569030055]),
 ('With the Union cabinet approving the amendments to the Motor Vehicles
Act, 2016, those caught for drunken driving will have to have really deep
pockets, as the fine payable in court has been enhanced to Rs 10,000 for
first-time offenders.',
```

```
  [0.18323712012013349]),
 ('Natural language processing (NLP) is an area of computer science and
artificial intelligence concerned with the interactions between computers
and human (natural) languages, in particular how to program computers to
process and analyze large amounts of natural language data.',
  [0.17995060855459855])]
```

Doc4 (on top in result) is most relevant to the query "cricket," even though the word cricket is not mentioned once, with a similarity of 0.449.

Let's take one more example as may be driving.

```
Ranked_documents("driving")
```

```
[('With the Union cabinet approving the amendments to the Motor Vehicles
Act, 2016, those caught for drunken driving will have to have really deep
pockets, as the fine payable in court has been enhanced to Rs 10,000 for
first-time offenders.',
  [0.35947287723800669]),
 ('But the man behind the wickets at the other end was watching just as
keenly. With an affirmative nod from Dhoni, India captain Rohit Sharma
promptly asked for a review. Sure enough, the ball would have clipped the
top of middle and leg.',
  [0.19042556935316801]),
 ('He points out that public transport is very good in Mumbai and New
Delhi, where there is a good network of suburban and metro rail systems.',
  [0.17066536985237601]),
 ('Natural language processing (NLP) is an area of computer science and
artificial intelligence concerned with the interactions between computers
and human (natural) languages, in particular how to program computers to
process and analyze large amounts of natural language data.',
  [0.088723080005327359])]
```

Again, since driving is connected to transport and the Motor Vehicles Act, it pulls out the most relevant documents on top. The first two documents are relevant to the query.

You can use the same approach and scale it up for as many documents as possible. For greater accuracy, you can build your own embeddings, as you learned in Chapter 3, for specific industries since the one we are using is generalized.

This is the fundamental approach that can be used for many applications like the following.

- Search engines

- Document retrieval

- Passage retrieval

- Question and answer

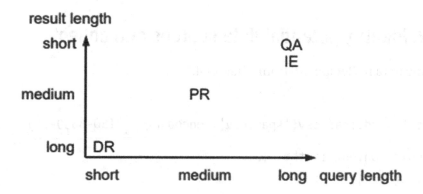

It's been proven that results are good when queries are longer and the resulting length is shorter. That's why you don't get great results in search engines when the search query has a lesser number of words.

Recipe 6-2. Classifying Text with Deep Learning

This recipe builds a text classifier using deep learning approaches.

Problem

You want to build a text classification model using CNN, RNN, and LSTM.

Solution

The approach and NLP pipeline remain the same. The only change is that instead of using machine learning algorithms, we are building models using deep learning algorithms.

How It Works

Follow the steps in this section to build the email classifier using the deep learning approaches.

Step 2-1. Define the business problem

Email classification (spam or ham). You need to classify spam or ham email based on email content.

Step 2-2. Identify potential data sources and collect

Use the same data in Recipe 4-6 from Chapter 4.

```
#read file
file_content = pd.read_csv('spam.csv', encoding = "ISO-8859-1")

#check sample content in the email
file_content['v2'][1]

#output
'Ok lar... Joking wif u oni...'
```

Step 2-3. Preprocess text

Let's preprocess the data.

```
#Import library
from nltk.corpus import stopwords
from nltk import *
from sklearn.feature_extraction.text import TfidfVectorizer
from nltk.stem import WordNetLemmatizer
import matplotlib.pyplot as plt
from sklearn.model_selection import train_test_split

# Remove stop words
stop = stopwords.words('english')
file_content['v2'] = file_content['v2'].apply(lambda x: " ".join(x for x in
x.split() if x not in stop))
```

```
# Delete unwanted columns
Email_Data = file_content[['v1', 'v2']]

# Rename column names
Email_Data = Email_Data.rename(columns={"v1":"Target", "v2":"Email"})
Email_Data.head()

#output
    Target Email
0   ham     Go jurong point, crazy.. Available bugis n gre...
1   ham     Ok lar... Joking wif u oni...
2   spam    Free entry 2 wkly comp win FA Cup final tkts 2...
3   ham     U dun say early hor... U c already say...
4   ham     Nah I think goes usf, lives around though

#Delete punctuations, convert text in lower case and delete the double space
Email_Data['Email'] = Email_Data['Email'].apply(lambda x:
re.sub('[!@#$:).;,?&]', '', x.lower()))
Email_Data['Email'] = Email_Data['Email'].apply(lambda x: re.sub('  ', ' ', x))
Email_Data['Email'].head(5)

#output
0 go jurong point crazy available bugis n great ...
1 ok lar joking wif u oni
2 free entry 2 wkly comp win fa cup final tkts 2...
3 u dun say early hor u c already say
4 nah i think goes usf lives around though
Name: Email, dtype: object

#Separating text(input) and target classes

list_sentences_rawdata = Email_Data["Email"].fillna("_na_").values
list_classes = ["Target"]
target = Email_Data[list_classes].values

To_Process=Email_Data[['Email', 'Target']]
```

Step 2-4. Prepare the data for model building

Next, prepare the data.

```
#Train and test split with 80:20 ratio
train, test = train_test_split(To_Process, test_size=0.2)

# Define the sequence lengths, max number of words and embedding dimensions
# Sequence length of each sentence. If more, truncate. If less, pad with
  zeros

MAX_SEQUENCE_LENGTH = 300 #user_transform

# Top 20000 frequently occurring words
MAX_NB_WORDS = 20000

# Get the frequently occurring words
 tokenizer = Tokenizer(num_words=MAX_NB_WORDS)
tokenizer.fit_on_texts(train.Email)
train_sequences = tokenizer.texts_to_sequences(train.Email)
test_sequences = tokenizer.texts_to_sequences(test.Email)

# dictionary containing words and their index
word_index = tokenizer.word_index
# print(tokenizer.word_index)
# total words in the corpus
print('Found %s unique tokens.' % len(word_index))

# get only the top frequent words on train
train_data = pad_sequences(train_sequences, maxlen=MAX_SEQUENCE_LENGTH)

# get only the top frequent words on test
test_data = pad_sequences(test_sequences, maxlen=MAX_SEQUENCE_LENGTH)

print(train_data.shape)
print(test_data.shape)

#output
Found 8443 unique tokens.
(4457, 300)
(1115, 300)
```

```
train_labels = train['Target']
test_labels = test['Target']

#import library
from sklearn.preprocessing import LabelEncoder
# converts the character array to numeric array. Assigns levels to unique
  labels.

le = LabelEncoder()
le.fit(train_labels)
train_labels = le.transform(train_labels)
test_labels = le.transform(test_labels)

print(le.classes_)
print(np.unique(train_labels, return_counts=True))
print(np.unique(test_labels, return_counts=True))

#output
['ham' 'spam']
(array([0, 1]), array([3889, 568]))
(array([0, 1]), array([936, 179]))

# changing data types
labels_train = to_categorical(np.asarray(train_labels))
labels_test = to_categorical(np.asarray(test_labels))
print('Shape of data tensor:', train_data.shape)
print('Shape of label tensor:', labels_train.shape)
print('Shape of label tensor:', labels_test.shape)

#output
Shape of data tensor: (4457, 300)
Shape of label tensor: (4457, 2)
Shape of label tensor: (1115, 2)

EMBEDDING_DIM = 100
print(MAX_SEQUENCE_LENGTH)

#output
300
```

Step 2-5. Model building and predicting

We are building the models using different deep learning approaches—like CNN, RNN, LSTM, and bidirectional LSTM—and comparing the performance of each model using different accuracy metrics. First, let's define the CNN model.

Here we define a single hidden layer with 128 memory units. The network uses a dropout with a probability of 0.5. The output layer is a dense layer using the softmax activation function to output a probability prediction.

```python
# Import Libraries
import sys, os, re, csv, codecs, numpy as np, pandas as pd

from keras.preprocessing.text import Tokenizer
from keras.preprocessing.sequence import pad_sequences
from keras.utils import to_categorical
from keras.layers import Dense, Input, LSTM, Embedding, Dropout, Activation
from keras.layers import Bidirectional, GlobalMaxPool1D, Conv1D, SimpleRNN
from keras.models import Model
from keras.models import Sequential
from keras import initializers, regularizers, constraints, optimizers, layers
from keras.layers import Dense, Input, Flatten, Dropout, BatchNormalization
from keras.layers import Conv1D, MaxPooling1D, Embedding
from keras.models import Sequential

 print('Training CNN 1D model.')
model = Sequential()
model.add(Embedding(MAX_NB_WORDS,
 EMBEDDING_DIM,
 input_length=MAX_SEQUENCE_LENGTH
 ))
model.add(Dropout(0.5))
model.add(Conv1D(128, 5, activation="relu"))
model.add(MaxPooling1D(5))
model.add(Dropout(0.5))
model.add(BatchNormalization())
model.add(Conv1D(128, 5, activation="relu"))
model.add(MaxPooling1D(5))
```

```
model.add(Dropout(0.5))
model.add(BatchNormalization())
model.add(Flatten())
model.add(Dense(128, activation="relu"))
model.add(Dense(2, activation="softmax"))

model.compile(loss='categorical_crossentropy',
 optimizer="rmsprop",
 metrics=['acc'])
```

We are now fitting our model to the data. There are five epochs and a batch size of 64 patterns.

```
model.fit(train_data, labels_train,
 batch_size=64,
 epochs=5,
 validation_data=(test_data, labels_test))
```

#output

```
Training CNN 1D model.
Train on 4457 samples, validate on 1115 samples
Epoch 1/5
4457/4457 [==============================] - 19s 4ms/step - loss: 0.3465 - acc: 0.8634 - val_loss: 0.3479 - val_acc:
0.9247
Epoch 2/5
4457/4457 [==============================] - 18s 4ms/step - loss: 0.1281 - acc: 0.9540 - val_loss: 0.1882 - val_acc:
0.9731
Epoch 3/5
4457/4457 [==============================] - 17s 4ms/step - loss: 0.0659 - acc: 0.9807 - val_loss: 0.5212 - val_acc:
0.9704
Epoch 4/5
4457/4457 [==============================] - 17s 4ms/step - loss: 0.0453 - acc: 0.9868 - val_loss: 0.5466 - val_acc:
0.9659
Epoch 5/5
4457/4457 [==============================] - 17s 4ms/step - loss: 0.0379 - acc: 0.9912 - val_loss: 0.5507 - val_acc:
0.9785

<keras.callbacks.History at 0x1a2df88f28>
```

#predictions on test data

```
predicted=model.predict(test_data)
predicted
```

#output
```
array([[0.5426713 , 0.45732868],
 [0.5431667 , 0.45683333],
 [0.53082496, 0.46917507],
 ...,
```

```
 [0.53582424, 0.46417573],
 [0.5305845 , 0.46941552],
 [0.53102577, 0.46897423]], dtype=float32)
```

#model evaluation

```
import sklearn
from sklearn.metrics import precision_recall_fscore_support as score

precision, recall, fscore, support = score(labels_test, predicted.round())

print('precision: {}'.format(precision))
print('recall: {}'.format(recall))
print('fscore: {}'.format(fscore))
print('support: {}'.format(support))

print("###########################")

print(sklearn.metrics.classification_report(labels_test, predicted.round()))
```

#output

```
          precision: [0.98407643 0.94797688]
          recall: [0.99038462 0.91620112]
          fscore: [0.98722045 0.93181818]
          support: [936 179]
          ###########################
                      precision    recall  f1-score   support

                 0        0.98      0.99      0.99       936
                 1        0.95      0.92      0.93       179

          avg / total    0.98      0.98      0.98      1115
```

We can now define our RNN model.

```
#import library
from keras.layers.recurrent import SimpleRNN

#model training

print('Training SIMPLERNN model.')

model = Sequential()
model.add(Embedding(MAX_NB_WORDS,
```

```
   EMBEDDING_DIM,
   input_length=MAX_SEQUENCE_LENGTH
   ))
model.add(SimpleRNN(2, input_shape=(None,1)))

model.add(Dense(2,activation='softmax'))

model.compile(loss = 'binary_crossentropy',
optimizer="adam",metrics = ['accuracy'])
model.fit(train_data, labels_train,
   batch_size=16,
   epochs=5,
   validation_data=(test_data, labels_test))

#output
```

```
Training SIMPLERNN  model.
Train on 4457 samples, validate on 1115 samples
Epoch 1/5
4457/4457 [==============================] - 26s 6ms/step - loss: 0.2514 - acc: 0.9607 - val_loss: 0.1508 - val_acc:
0.9776
Epoch 2/5
4457/4457 [==============================] - 25s 6ms/step - loss: 0.0768 - acc: 0.9917 - val_loss: 0.1013 - val_acc:
0.9785
Epoch 3/5
4457/4457 [==============================] - 25s 6ms/step - loss: 0.0327 - acc: 0.9982 - val_loss: 0.0904 - val_acc:
0.9794
Epoch 4/5
4457/4457 [==============================] - 25s 6ms/step - loss: 0.0171 - acc: 0.9996 - val_loss: 0.0920 - val_acc:
0.9767
Epoch 5/5
4457/4457 [==============================] - 25s 6ms/step - loss: 0.0108 - acc: 1.0000 - val_loss: 0.0926 - val_acc:
0.9749
```

```
# prediction on test data
predicted_Srnn=model.predict(test_data)
predicted_Srnn

#output
array([[0.9959137 , 0.00408628],
  [0.99576926, 0.00423072],
  [0.99044365, 0.00955638],
  ...,
  [0.9920791 , 0.00792089],
  [0.9958105 , 0.00418955],
  [0.99660563, 0.00339443]], dtype=float32)

#model evaluation
```

235

```
from sklearn.metrics import precision_recall_fscore_support as score

precision, recall, fscore, support = score(labels_test, predicted_Srnn.round())

print('precision: {}'.format(precision))
print('recall: {}'.format(recall))
print('fscore: {}'.format(fscore))
print('support: {}'.format(support))

print("##########################")

print(sklearn.metrics.classification_report(labels_test,
predicted_Srnn.round()))

#output
```

```
        precision: [0.97589099 0.9689441 ]
        recall: [0.99465812 0.87150838]
        fscore: [0.98518519 0.91764706]
        support: [936 179]
        ##########################
                    precision    recall  f1-score   support

               0        0.98      0.99      0.99       936
               1        0.97      0.87      0.92       179

       avg / total      0.97      0.97      0.97      1115
```

And here is our long short-term memory (LSTM) model.

```
#model training

print('Training LSTM model.')

model = Sequential()
model.add(Embedding(MAX_NB_WORDS,
 EMBEDDING_DIM,
 input_length=MAX_SEQUENCE_LENGTH
 ))
model.add(LSTM(output_dim=16, activation="relu",
inner_activation="hard_sigmoid",return_sequences=True))
model.add(Dropout(0.2))
```

```
model.add(BatchNormalization())
model.add(Flatten())

model.add(Dense(2,activation='softmax'))

model.compile(loss = 'binary_crossentropy', optimizer="adam",metrics =
['accuracy'])

model.fit(train_data, labels_train,
 batch_size=16,
 epochs=5,
 validation_data=(test_data, labels_test))

#output
```

```
Training LSTM  model.
/Users/akulk7/anaconda/lib/python3.5/site-packages/ipykernel/__main__.py:12: UserWarning: Update your `LSTM` call to
the Keras 2 API: `LSTM(recurrent_activation="hard_sigmoid", return_sequences=True, units=16, activation="relu")`
Train on 4457 samples, validate on 1115 samples
Epoch 1/5
4457/4457 [==============================] - 75s 17ms/step - loss: 0.1260 - acc: 0.9587 - val_loss: 0.1605 - val_acc:
0.9596
Epoch 2/5
4457/4457 [==============================] - 72s 16ms/step - loss: 0.0147 - acc: 0.9964 - val_loss: 0.0810 - val_acc:
0.9794
Epoch 3/5
4457/4457 [==============================] - 72s 16ms/step - loss: 0.0028 - acc: 0.9991 - val_loss: 0.0968 - val_acc:
0.9812
Epoch 4/5
4457/4457 [==============================] - 73s 16ms/step - loss: 0.0018 - acc: 0.9998 - val_loss: 0.0892 - val_acc:
0.9830
Epoch 5/5
4457/4457 [==============================] - 78s 17ms/step - loss: 7.3629e-04 - acc: 0.9998 - val_loss: 0.1045 - val_
acc: 0.9830
```

```
#prediction on text data
predicted_lstm=model.predict(test_data)
predicted_lstm
array([[1.0000000e+00, 4.0581045e-09],
 [1.0000000e+00, 8.3188789e-13],
 [9.9999976e-01, 1.8647323e-07],
 ...,
 [9.9999976e-01, 1.8333606e-07],
 [1.0000000e+00, 1.7347950e-09],
 [9.9999988e-01, 1.3574694e-07]], dtype=float32)

#model evaluation
```

```
from sklearn.metrics import precision_recall_fscore_support as score

precision, recall, fscore, support = score(labels_test,
predicted_lstm.round())

print('precision: {}'.format(precision))
print('recall: {}'.format(recall))
print('fscore: {}'.format(fscore))
print('support: {}'.format(support))

print("###########################")

print(sklearn.metrics.classification_report(labels_test,
predicted_lstm.round()))

#output
```

```
              precision: [0.98010471 1.          ]
              recall: [1.            0.89385475]
              fscore: [0.98995241 0.9439528 ]
              support: [936 179]
              ###########################
                        precision    recall   f1-score    support

                    0       0.98       1.00       0.99        936
                    1       1.00       0.89       0.94        179

           avg / total      0.98       0.98       0.98       1115
```

Finally, let's discuss bidirectional LSTM and implement it.

LSTM preserves information from inputs using the hidden state. In bidirectional LSTMs, inputs are fed in two ways: one from past to future and the other going backward from future to past, helping to learn future representations. Bidirectional LSTMs are known for producing very good results because they can understand the context better.

```
#model training

print('Training Bidirectional LSTM model.')

model = Sequential()
model.add(Embedding(MAX_NB_WORDS,
 EMBEDDING_DIM,
 input_length=MAX_SEQUENCE_LENGTH
 ))
```

```
model.add(Bidirectional(LSTM(16, return_sequences=True, dropout=0.1,
recurrent_dropout=0.1)))
model.add(Conv1D(16, kernel_size = 3, padding = "valid",
kernel_initializer = "glorot_uniform"))
model.add(GlobalMaxPool1D())
model.add(Dense(50, activation="relu"))
model.add(Dropout(0.1))

model.add(Dense(2,activation='softmax'))

model.compile(loss = 'binary_crossentropy', optimizer="adam",metrics =
['accuracy'])

model.fit(train_data, labels_train,
 batch_size=16,
 epochs=3,
 validation_data=(test_data, labels_test))
```

#output

```
Training Bidirectional LSTM  model.
Train on 4457 samples, validate on 1115 samples
Epoch 1/3
4457/4457 [==============================] - 104s 23ms/step - loss: 0.1401 - acc: 0.9502 - val_loss: 0.0669 - val_ac
c: 0.9821
Epoch 2/3
4457/4457 [==============================] - 99s 22ms/step - loss: 0.0119 - acc: 0.9960 - val_loss: 0.0776 - val_acc:
0.9812
Epoch 3/3
4457/4457 [==============================] - 100s 22ms/step - loss: 0.0020 - acc: 0.9998 - val_loss: 0.0890 - val_ac
c: 0.9857
```

prediction on test data

```
predicted_blstm=model.predict(test_data)
predicted_blstm
```

#output
```
array([[9.9999976e-01, 2.6086647e-07],
 [9.9999809e-01, 1.9633851e-06],
 [9.9999833e-01, 1.6918856e-06],
 ...,
 [9.9999273e-01, 7.2622524e-06],
 [9.9999964e-01, 3.3541210e-07],
```

```
 [9.9999964e-01, 3.5427794e-07]], dtype=float32)
```

```python
#model evaluation

from sklearn.metrics import precision_recall_fscore_support as score

precision, recall, fscore, support = score(labels_test,
predicted_blstm.round())

print('precision: {}'.format(precision))
print('recall: {}'.format(recall))
print('fscore: {}'.format(fscore))
print('support: {}'.format(support))

print("###########################")

print(sklearn.metrics.classification_report(labels_test,
predicted_blstm.round()))

#output
```

```
precision: [0.98421053 0.99393939]
recall: [0.99893162 0.91620112]
fscore: [0.99151644 0.95348837]
support: [936 179]
###########################
             precision    recall  f1-score   support

         0       0.98      1.00      0.99       936
         1       0.99      0.92      0.95       179

avg / total       0.99      0.99      0.99      1115
```

You can see that bidirectional LSTM outperforms the rest of the algorithms.

Recipe 6-3. Next Word Prediction

Autofill/show the potential sequence of words saves a lot of time while writing emails and makes users happy to use it in any product.

Problem

You want to build a model to predict/suggest the next word based on a previous sequence of words using email data.

Like you see in the below image, language is being suggested as the next word.

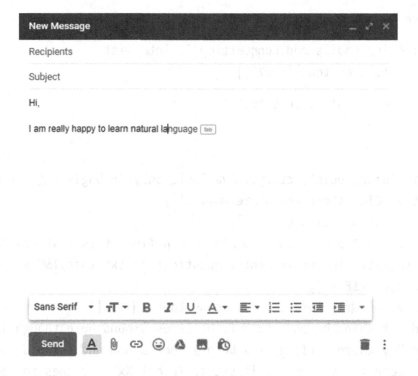

Solution

This section builds an LSTM model to learn sequences of words from email data. This model predicts the next word.

How It Works

Follow the steps in this section to build the next word prediction model using the deep learning approach.

Step 3-1. Define the business problem

Predict the next word based on the sequence of words or sentences.

Step 3-2. Identify potential data sources and collect

For this problem, let's use the same email data from Recipe 4-6 in Chapter 4. This has a lot less data, but still, to showcase the working flow, we are fine with this data. The more data, the better the accuracy.

```
file_content = pd.read_csv('spam.csv', encoding = "ISO-8859-1")

# Just selecting emails and connverting it into list
Email_Data = file_content[[ 'v2']]

list_data = Email_Data.values.tolist()
list_data

#output
[['Go until jurong point, crazy.. Available only in bugis n great world la
  e buffet... Cine there got amore wat...'],
 ['Ok lar... Joking wif u oni...'],
 ["Free entry in 2 a wkly comp to win FA Cup final tkts 21st May 2005.
  Text FA to 87121 to receive entry question(std txt rate)T&C's apply
  08452810075over18's"],
 ['U dun say so early hor... U c already then say...'],
 ["Nah I don't think he goes to usf, he lives around here though"],
 ["FreeMsg Hey there darling it's been 3 week's now and no word back!
  I'd like some fun you up for it still? Tb ok! XxX std chgs to send,
  å£1.50 to rcv"],
 ['Even my brother is not like to speak with me. They treat me like aids
  patent.'],
 ["As per your request 'Melle Melle (Oru Minnaminunginte Nurungu Vettam)'
  has been set as your callertune for all Callers. Press *9 to copy your
  friends Callertune"],
 ['WINNER!! As a valued network customer you have been selected to receivea
  å£900 prize reward! To claim call 09061701461. Claim code KL341. Valid 12
  hours only.'] ,
 ['Had your mobile 11 months or more? U R entitled to Update to the latest
  colour mobiles with camera for Free! Call The Mobile Update Co FREE on
  08002986030'],
```

Step 3-3. Import and install necessary libraries

Here are the libraries.

```
import numpy as np
import random
import pandas as pd
import sys
import os
import time
import codecs
import collections
import numpy
from keras.models import Sequential
from keras.layers import Dense
from keras.layers import Dropout
from keras.layers import LSTM
from keras.callbacks import ModelCheckpoint
from keras.utils import np_utils
from nltk.tokenize import sent_tokenize, word_tokenize
import scipy
from scipy import spatial
from nltk.tokenize.toktok import ToktokTokenizer
import re
tokenizer = ToktokTokenizer()
```

Step 3-4. Process the data

Next, process the data.

```
#Converting list to string
from collections import Iterable

def flatten(items):
    """Yield items from any nested iterable"""
    for x in items:
        if isinstance(x, Iterable) and not isinstance(x, (str, bytes)):
            for sub_x in flatten(x):
```

```
            yield sub_x
      else:
          yield x

TextData=list(flatten(list_data))
TextData = ".join(TextData)

# Remove unwanted lines and converting into lower case
TextData = TextData.replace('\n',")
TextData = TextData.lower()

pattern = r'[^a-zA-z0-9\s]'
TextData = re.sub(pattern, ", ".join(TextData))

# Tokenizing
tokens = tokenizer.tokenize(TextData)
tokens = [token.strip() for token in tokens]

# get the distinct words and sort it

word_counts = collections.Counter(tokens)
word_c = len(word_counts)

print(word_c)

distinct_words = [x[0] for x in word_counts.most_common()]
distinct_words_sorted = list(sorted(distinct_words))

# Generate indexing for all words

word_index = {x: i for i, x in enumerate(distinct_words_sorted)}

# decide on sentence length

sentence_length = 25
```

Step 3-5. Prepare data for modeling

This step divides the mail into a sequence of words with a fixed length of ten words. (You can choose anything based on the business problem and computation power.) The text is split by word sequences. When creating these sequences, this window slides along the whole document one word at a time, allowing each word to learn from the preceding one.

```
#prepare the dataset of input to output pairs encoded as integers
# Generate the data for the model

#input = the input sentence to the model with index
#output = output of the model with index

InputData = []
OutputData = []

for i in range(0, word_c - sentence_length, 1):
    X = tokens[i:i + sentence_length]
    Y = tokens[i + sentence_length]
    InputData.append([word_index[char] for char in X])
    OutputData.append(word_index[Y])

print (InputData[:1])
print ("\n")
print(OutputData[:1])

#output

[[5086, 12190, 6352, 9096, 3352, 1920, 8507, 5937, 2535, 7886, 5214, 12910, 6541,
4104, 2531, 2997, 11473, 5170, 1595, 12552, 6590, 6316, 12758, 12087, 8496]]

[4292]

# Generate  X
X = numpy.reshape(InputData, (len(InputData), sentence_length, 1))

# One hot encode the output variable
Y = np_utils.to_categorical(OutputData)

Y
#output
array([[0., 0., 0., ..., 0., 0., 0.],
       [0., 0., 0., ..., 0., 0., 0.],
       [0., 0., 0., ..., 0., 0., 0.],
       ...,
       [0., 0., 0., ..., 0., 0., 0.],
       [0., 0., 0., ..., 0., 0., 0.],
       [0., 0., 0., ..., 0., 0., 0.]])
```

Step 3-6. Build the model

Next, let's define the LSTM model, a single hidden LSTM layer with 256 memory units. This model uses dropout 0.2. The output layer uses the softmax activation function. Here we use the ADAM optimizer.

```
# define the LSTM model
model = Sequential()
model.add(LSTM(256, input_shape=(X.shape[1], X.shape[2])))
model.add(Dropout(0.2))
model.add(Dense(Y.shape[1], activation="softmax"))
model.compile(loss='categorical_crossentropy', optimizer="adam")

#define the checkpoint
file_name_path="weights-improvement-{epoch:02d}-{loss:.4f}.hdf5"
checkpoint = ModelCheckpoint(file_name_path, monitor="loss", verbose=1,
save_best_only=True, mode="min")
callbacks = [checkpoint]
```

You can now fit the model to the data. Here we use five epochs and a batch size of 128 patterns. For better results, you can use more epochs like 50 or 100. And of course, you can use them on more data.

```
#fit the model
model.fit(X, Y, epochs=5, batch_size=128, callbacks=callbacks)
```

Note   We have not split the data into training and testing data. We are not interested in the accurate model. Deep learning models require a lot of data for training and take a lot of time to train, so we are using a model checkpoint to capture all the model weights to file. We use the best set of weights for our prediction.

```
#output
```

```
Epoch 1/5
13312/13335 [============================>.] - ETA: 0s - loss: 7.9041
Epoch 00001: loss improved from inf to 7.90363, saving model to weights-improvement-01-7.9036.hdf5
13335/13335 [=============================] - 30s 2ms/step - loss: 7.9036
Epoch 2/5
13312/13335 [============================>.] - ETA: 0s - loss: 7.1114
Epoch 00002: loss improved from 7.90363 to 7.11067, saving model to weights-improvement-02-7.1107.hdf5
13335/13335 [=============================] - 28s 2ms/step - loss: 7.1107
Epoch 3/5
13312/13335 [============================>.] - ETA: 0s - loss: 7.0211
Epoch 00003: loss improved from 7.11067 to 7.02179, saving model to weights-improvement-03-7.0218.hdf5
13335/13335 [=============================] - 26s 2ms/step - loss: 7.0218
Epoch 4/5
13312/13335 [============================>.] - ETA: 0s - loss: 6.9316
Epoch 00004: loss improved from 7.02179 to 6.93116, saving model to weights-improvement-04-6.9312.hdf5
13335/13335 [=============================] - 26s 2ms/step - loss: 6.9312
Epoch 5/5
13312/13335 [============================>.] - ETA: 0s - loss: 6.8516
Epoch 00005: loss improved from 6.93116 to 6.85182, saving model to weights-improvement-05-6.8518.hdf5
13335/13335 [=============================] - 28s 2ms/step - loss: 6.8518
```

After running the code, you have weight checkpoint files in your local directory. Pick the network weights file that is saved in your working directory. When we ran this example, we got the following checkpoint with the smallest loss that we achieved with five epochs.

```
# load the network weights
file_name = "weights-improvement-05-6.8213.hdf5"
model.load_weights(file_name)
model.compile(loss='categorical_crossentropy', optimizer="adam")
```

Step 3-7. Predict the next word

Randomly generate a sequence of words and input to the model and see what it predicts.

```
# Generating random sequence
start = numpy.random.randint(0, len(InputData))
input_sent = InputData[start]

# Generate index of the next word of the email

X = numpy.reshape(input_sent, (1, len(input_sent), 1))

predict_word = model.predict(X, verbose=0)
index = numpy.argmax(predict_word)

print(input_sent)
print ("\n")
print(index)
```

247

```
# Output
[9122, 1920, 8187, 5905, 6828, 9818, 1791, 5567, 1597, 7092, 11606, 7466,
 10198, 6105, 1837, 4752, 7092, 3928, 10347, 5849, 8816, 7092, 8574, 7092,
 1831]

5849

# Convert these indexes back to words

word_index_rev = dict((i, c) for i, c in enumerate(tokens))
result = word_index_rev[index]
sent_in = [word_index_rev[value] for value in input_sent]

print(sent_in)
print ("\n")
print(result)
```

Result :

```
['us', 'came', 'use', 'respecthe', 'would', 'us', 'are', 'it', 'you', 'to',
 'pray', 'because', 'you', 'do', 'me', 'out', 'youre', 'thk', 'where',
 'are', 'mrng', 'minutes', 'long', '500', 'per']
```

shut

So, given the 25 input words, it's predicting the word "shut" as the next word. Of course, its not making much sense, since it has been trained on much less data and epochs. Make sure you have great computation power and train on huge data with high number of epochs.

Recipe 6-4. Stack Overflow question recommendation

Stack Overflow is a question-and-answer website for professionals and enthusiast developers. *It* is the largest online community for programmers to learn, share their knowledge, and build their careers

Problem

Every day thousands of questions are asked and answered in the Stack Overflow community. There is a high chance that the same type of questions is asked, which creates unnecessary duplicate questions in the system. If the system can recommend a similar question when the user asks a new question, that reduces the significant duplication.

Solution

We need to compare the question asked with all the rest of the existing questions. This is a sentence comparison task. We are using pre-trained embeddings to obtain sentence-level average vectors to calculate the similarity scores. These scores are then used to rank the questions.

Let's use various pre-trained models like BERT sentence-transformers, Open AI–GPT, and GloVe to solve this project and a traditional TFIDF approach.

How It Works

Step 4-1. Collect data

Use the free source dataset where there are Stack Overflow questions. The raw data set is at `www.kaggle.com/c/predict-closed-questions-on-stack-overflow/data?select=train-sample.csv`.

Download this dataset and save it in a folder for further use.

Step 4-2. Import Notebook and data to Google Colab

Google Colab is used to solve this project given BERT models are large, and building it in Colab is easier and faster.

Go to Google Colab (`https://colab.research.google.com/notebooks/intro.ipynb`).

Then go to File and open a new notebook or Upload notebook from local using "Upload notebook". Follow below screenshot.

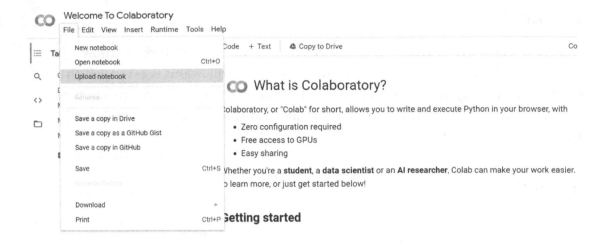

To import the data, go to Files, and click the "Upload to session storage" option. Example is shown in below image.

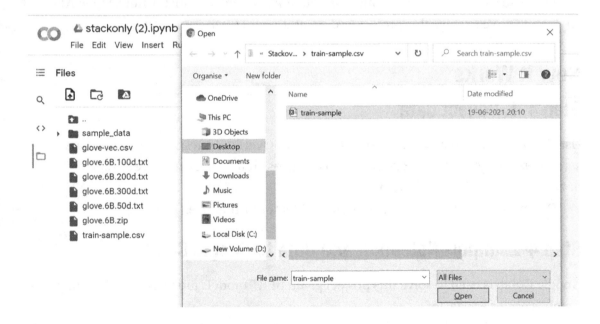

Step 4-3. Import the libraries

Let's import the necessary libraries.

```
#importing necessary libraries
import pandas as pd
import numpy as np
```

```
import pickle
import time

import re
from bs4 import BeautifulSoup
import nltk
from nltk.tokenize import ToktokTokenizer
from nltk.stem.wordnet import WordNetLemmatizer

from string import punctuation
import matplotlib.pyplot as plt
import nltk
nltk.download('stopwords')
from nltk.corpus import stopwords
from sklearn.feature_extraction.text import TfidfVectorizer
import re
from nltk.stem.porter import PorterStemmer
from nltk.stem import WordNetLemmatizer

from sklearn.metrics.pairwise import cosine_similarity
from scipy.sparse import coo_matrix, hstack,csr_matrix
```

Step 4-4. Import the data and EDA

Let's import the data and do some quick EDA before solving the actual problem.

```
#importing training data
df=pd.read_csv('train-sample.csv')

#counting all null values

df.isnull().sum()
```

```
PostId                                        0
PostCreationDate                              0
OwnerUserId                                   0
OwnerCreationDate                             0
ReputationAtPostCreation                      0
OwnerUndeletedAnswerCountAtPostTime           0
```

```
Title                                   0
BodyMarkdown                            0
Tag1                                   10
Tag2                                27251
Tag3                                64358
Tag4                               100622
Tag5                               124558
PostClosedDate                      70136
OpenStatus                              0
dtype: int64
```

```
#Replacing missing values with blank space

df['Tag1']=df['Tag1'].replace(np.NaN,'')
df['Tag2']=df['Tag2'].replace(np.NaN,'')
df['Tag3']=df['Tag3'].replace(np.NaN,'')
df['Tag4']=df['Tag4'].replace(np.NaN,'')
df['Tag5']=df['Tag5'].replace(np.NaN,'')
```

```
#converting column type into string

df['Title']=df['Title'].astype(str)
df['BodyMarkdown']=df['BodyMarkdown'].astype(str)
```

```
#checking top 10 most common words from the Body column

from collections import Counter
cnt = Counter()
for text in df["BodyMarkdown"].values:
    for word in text.split():
        cnt[word] += 1
```

```
cnt.most_common(10)  #top 10 common words
```

```
# Result

[('the', 514615),
 ('to', 410003),
 ('I', 358442),
 ('a', 285706),
```

```
('and', 212914),
('is', 192019),
('in', 182699),
('=', 180765),
('of', 164698),
('that', 121863)]
```

These are stop words and are removed in data cleaning steps.

Step 4-5. Clean the text data

Let's do some standard data cleaning processes.

```
#importing tokenizer for sentence tokenization
token=ToktokTokenizer()

#stop words removing function
def stopWords(text):

    stop_words = set(stopwords.words("english"))   #importing stopwords
                                                    dictionary

    #text = re.sub('[^a-zA-Z]', ' ', text)
    words=token.tokenize(text)                       # tokenizing sentences

    filtered = [w for w in words if not w in stop_words] #filtering words
                                                          which are not in
                                                          stopwords

    return ' '.join(map(str, filtered))   #creating string combining all
                                           filtered words

#function to remove punctuations
def remove_punctuations(text):
    punct = '!"#$%&\'()*+,./:;<=>?@[\\]^_`{|}~'    #list of punctuation marks
    for punctuation in punct:
        text = text.replace(punctuation, '')    #replacing punctuation mark
                                                 with blank space

    return text
```

```python
#function to remove frequent words but they were mostly from stopwords
FREQWORDS = set([w for (w, wc) in cnt.most_common(10)])
def remove_freqwords(text):

    return " ".join([word for word in str(text).split() if word not in
    FREQWORDS])

#cleaning the text

def clean_text(text):
    text = text.lower()
    text = re.sub(r"what's", "what is ", text)
    text = re.sub(r"\'s", " ", text)
    text = re.sub(r"n't", " not ", text)
    text = re.sub(r"i'm", "i am ", text)
    text = re.sub(r"\'re", " are ", text)
    text = re.sub(r"\'d", " would ", text)
    text = re.sub(r"\'ll", " will ", text)
    text = re.sub(r"\'scuse", " excuse ", text)
    text = re.sub(r"\'\n", " ", text)
    text = re.sub('\s+', ' ', text)
    text = re.sub(r"\'ve", " have ", text)x`
    text = re.sub(r"can't", "can not ", text)
    text = text.strip(' ')
    return text

#URL removing function
def remove_urls(text):
    url_pattern = re.compile(r'https?://\S+|www\.\S+')
    return url_pattern.sub(r'', text)

#function to remove html tag and replacing with blank space
def remove_html(text):
    html_pattern = re.compile('<.*?>')
    return html_pattern.sub(r'', text)
```

Let's use the above created functions on the BodyMarkdown column in the dataset.

```
#Applying all preprocessing steps defined above on both Body

df['BodyMarkdown']=df['BodyMarkdown'].apply(lambda x: clean_text(x))
df['BodyMarkdown'] = df['BodyMarkdown'].apply(remove_punctuations)
df['BodyMarkdown'] = df['BodyMarkdown'].apply(remove_urls)
df['BodyMarkdown'] = df['BodyMarkdown'].apply(remove_html)
df['BodyMarkdown'] = df['BodyMarkdown'].apply(lambda x:stopWords(x))
```

Step 4-6. Use TFIDF for feature engineering

There are various ways to convert text to features. Let's start with TFIDF.

```
#Importing TFIDF vector as tfidf_vectorizer

tfidf_vectorizer = TfidfVectorizer()

#applying tfidf on Body  column


tfidf_matrix2 = tfidf_vectorizer.fit_transform(df['BodyMarkdown'])
```

This matrix is used later to fetch similar questions.

Step 4-7. Use GloVe embeddings for feature engineering

Let's import the GloVe pre-trained model.

```
!wget http://nlp.stanford.edu/data/glove.6B.zip
!unzip glove*.zip
!ls
!pwd
```

Note   Extracting and calculating the average vector takes hours.

Extracting features for the whole dataset takes a lot of time. First, consider less number of samples for development and testing the code. Once everything is working, consider the whole dataset to extract features and find similar questions.

```
#creating sample data set with 100 rows for testing. Comment this line to
run it on the whole dataset.

dfg=df.iloc[0:100,:]

# load the glove model

glove_model = pd.read_table("glove.6B.100d.txt", sep=" ", index_col=0,
header=None, quoting=csv.QUOTE_NONE)

# getting mean vector for each sentence

def get_mean_vector(glove_model, words):
    # remove out-of-vocabulary words
    words = [word for word in word_tokenize(words) if word in
    list(glove_model.index)] #if word is in vocab
    if len(words) >= 1:
        return np.mean(glove_model.loc[words].values, axis=0)
    else:
        return np.array([0]*100)

#Defining empty list and appending array to the list

glove_embeddings=[]
for i in dfg.BodyMarkdown:
    glove_embeddings.append(list(get_mean_vector(glove_model, i)))
```

The *glove_embeddings* have the vector for all the sentences in the dataset. Run this once and save the vectors to avoid running it every time since it takes a lot of time.

Let's export this into a CSV file so that you can utilize it whenever required.

```
# Saving vectors of each abstract in the #data frame so that we can use
them directly while running code again

glove_embeddings_t=pd.DataFrame(K1).transpose()
glove_embeddings_t.to_csv('glove-vec.csv')
```

The following code imports the CSV file, which has the vectors we just exported. When the new session is opened, you need to run the code to load the vectors for this dataset.

```
#Loading our pre-trained vectors of each abstract

K=pd.read_csv('glove-vec.csv')
glove_embeddings_loaded=[]

#transforming data frame into a required array-#like structure as we did in
the above step

for i in range(dfg.shape[0]):
  glove_embeddings_loaded.append(K[str(i)].values)
glove_embeddings_loaded=np.asarray(glove_embeddings_loaded)
```

Step 4-8. Use GPT for feature engineering

Let's install Open AI's GPT model.

```
!pip install pytorch_pretrained_bert

# importing necessary libraries for GPT

import torch
from pytorch_pretrained_bert import OpenAIGPTTokenizer, OpenAIGPTModel

tokenizer = OpenAIGPTTokenizer.from_pretrained('openai-gpt')
model = OpenAIGPTModel.from_pretrained('openai-gpt')
model.eval()
print('Model Loaded')

#function to get embedding of each token
def returnEmbedding(pSentence):
  tokens = pSentence.split(' ')
  hidden_states = np.zeros((1,768))
  for token in tokens:
      subwords = tokenizer.tokenize(token)
      indexed_tokens = tokenizer.convert_tokens_to_ids(subwords)
      tokens_tensor = torch.tensor([indexed_tokens])

      with torch.no_grad():
          try:
            hidden_states += np.array(torch.mean(model(tokens_tensor),1))
```

```
        except Exception as ex:
            continue
    hidden_states /= len(tokens)
    return hidden_states
```

```
# Initialize Matrix with number of dataset records as rows and 768 columns
as embedding dimension
X = np.zeros((df_gpt.shape[0], 768))
```

```
# Generate sentence level embedding by calculating average of all word
embedding
for iter in range(df_gpt.shape[0]):
    text = df_gpt.loc[iter,'BodyMarkdown']
    #print(iter)
    X[iter] = returnEmbedding(text)
```

```
embeddings_GPT = X
```

The embeddings_GPT is used later to find the top n similar questions.

Step 4-9. Use Sentence-BERT for feature engineering

```
# Install BERT sentence transformer for sentence encoding
!pip install sentence-transformers
```

```
#running on 100 rows only for testing. Later comment this line
df_bert=df.iloc[0:100,:]
```

```
#importing bert-base model
```

```
from sentence_transformers import SentenceTransformer
sbert_model = SentenceTransformer('bert-base-nli-mean-tokens')
```

```
#embeding on Body column
sentence_embeddings = sbert_model.encode(df['BodyMarkdown'])
print('Sample BERT embedding vector - length', len(sentence_embeddings[0]))
```

```
#output
Sample BERT embedding vector - length 768
```

Step 4-10. Create functions to fetch top questions

Now that we have extracted vectors or embeddings for each question in the dataset, let's create functions to

- Find cosine similarities

- Return top n similar questions (ranking)

```
#defining function to derive cosine similarity
from numpy import dot
from numpy.linalg import norm
def cos_sim(a,b):

    return dot(a, b)/(norm(a)*norm(b))
```

```
#Function which returns Top N similar sentence from data frame directly

def top_n(user,p,df):

    #Converting cosine similarities of overall data set with input queries
    into LIST
    x=cosine_similarity(user,p).tolist()[0]

 #store list in temp file to retrieve index
    tmp=list(x)

#sort the list
    x.sort(reverse=True)

    print( x[0:5])

#get index of top 5
    L=[]
    for i in x[0:5]:

        L.append(tmp.index(i))
    return df.iloc[L, [6,7]]
```

These two functions and all the embeddings are used in the next section.

Step 4-11. Preprocess user input

Users can input any question. You need to preprocess the user input text and extract the embeddings based on one type of model selected. The following function does this.

```
#function to pre-process and extract embeddings for the user input text

def user_transform(query,model):
    query= clean_text(query)
    query= remove_punctuations(query)
    query= remove_urls(query)
    query= remove_html(query)
    query= stopWords(query)
    print(query)
    if model=='TFIDF':
      k=tfidf_vectorizer.transform([str(query)])
    elif model=='BERT':
      k=sbert_model.encode(str(query))
    elif model=='glove_model':
      k=get_mean_vector(glove_model,query)
      k=k.reshape(1,-1)
    elif model=='GPT':
      k=returnEmbedding(query)

    return k

 pd.set_option("display.max_colwidth", -1)
        #this function will display full text from each column
```

Step 4-12. Find similar questions

Find similar questions using TFIDF.

```
# Getting top 5 similar questions for user input query using TFIDF

input=user_transform('do we have any other Q&A platform like stackoverflow
which is free source?','TFIDF')

top_n(input,tfidf_matrix2,df)
```

	Title	BodyMarkdown
93	Is there an open source Q&A platform similar to stackoverflow?	I need a good open source Q&A platform to boost collective intelligence of my community. The stackoverflow workflow is perfect for me. Do you know of any similar platform?
18320	what is a platform and what is an application?	When do you call something that you are building a platform and when is it just a simple application? \r\n\r\nWhat are some of the examples of a platform?

If you look at the results, the first question is similar to the one user input query.
Find similar questions using GloVe.

```
# Getting top 5 similar questions using Glove model

input=user_transform('do we have any other Q&A platform like stackoverflow
which is free source?','glove_model')   #query

top_n(input,glove_embeddings_loaded,df)
```

	Title	BodyMarkdown
93	Is there an open source Q&A platform similar to stackoverflow?	I need a good open source Q&A platform to boost collective intelligence of my community. The stackoverflow workflow is perfect for me. Do you know of any similar platform?
58	Audio Stream URLs and Problem Solving Stream URLs	I thought I would share what I went through. This is not a question. We solved a problem. I'm sure old media server hounds know about this. I didn't. I hope this saves you time in the future.\r\n\r\nProblem: My customer's Shoutcast listing went away but their provider didn't. (Shoutcast has listings for many stations as a convenience. My customer's used to be: \r\nhttp: //yp.shoutcast.com/sbin/tunein-station.pls?id=3012xxx and then it went away! Their station didn't.\r\n\r\nWe were left with several URLs provided us by the station and none of them played via our player. Within each .pls, .ram file, the same URL was listed (see note) - something like this:\r\n\r\nhttp: //74.53.186.162:9082/\r\n\r\nHow did we solve the problem?\r\n\r\nOn the Shoutcast console page above, there is a listen link. It refers to a URL with a .pls extension. It also shows the sample rate, number of current listeners, etc. The URL worked. \r\n\r\nWhat made this interesting is that file located at that URL actually was a .pls text file with the original URL (something like http: //74.53.186.162:9082/) !\r\n\r\nWhat did I learn?\r\n\r\n1. Shoutcast servers know what kind of client is accessing their data. I would assume the same to be true of IceCast servers. How did I know? The circular URL reference. This means that your player parses text files first much like your browser looks at the mime type.\r\n2. Media player classes that you use in code can be really dumb. They're sensitive to mime types, bit rates, extension names, etc.\r\n3. If I have the .pls or other media file, I can use them locally.\r\n4. Hard coded IP addresses are just as bad as they ever were. Unfortunately, developers don't have much control over this.\r\n\r\nNote: Audio Streams with .pls, .ram, etc are text files that have URLs in them to the actual stream. The text file has other meta data as well. If you take the raw URL from the txt file and launch It, you might get a Shoutcast Server interface that gives you stream information that your player might use. (When viewing a radio station's website, you can sometimes find the stream URL in the player's launch parms. Sometimes they can be different.)

If you look at the results, the first question is similar to the one user input query.
Find similar questions using GPT.

```
#similar questions from GPT (from 100 rows)

input=user_transform('do we have any other Q&A platform like stackoverflow
which is free source?','GPT')   #query

top_n(input,embeddings_GPT,df)
```

	Title	BodyMarkdown
77	Option menu default gray border removal	In my app i have option menu I try to customize it , i did it by refer it to style ,\r\n\r\nwhat i need is either removal of default gray border around option menu or customize it to another color .\r\n\r\nany advice will be appreciated . \r\n\r\n\r\nas shown below :\r\n\r\n![enter image description here][1]\r\n\r\n My code :\r\n\r\n public boolean onCreateOptionsMenu(android.view.Menu menu) {\r\n\t\r\n\t MenuInflater inflater = getMenuInflater();\r\n\t inflater.inflate(R.menu.cool_menu, menu);\r\n\r\n\t getLayoutInflater().setFactory(new Factory() {\r\n\t public View onCreateView(String name, Context context,\r\n\t AttributeSet attrs) {\r\n\t\tif (name .equalsIgnoreCase("com.android.internal.view.menu.IconMenuItemView")) {\r\n\t\try {\r\n\t\r\n\t LayoutInflater li = LayoutInflater.from(context);\r\n\t final View view = li.createView(name, null, attrs);\r\n\t\r\n\t new Handler().post(new Runnable() {\r\n\t public void run() {\r\n\t\r\n\t view .setBackgroundResource(R.drawable.border1);\r\n\t\r\n\t ((TextView) view).setTextSize(20); \r\n\t\r\n\t ((TextView) view).setTextColor(Color.RED);\r\n\t }\r\n\t });\r\n\t return view; }\r\n\t catch (InflateException e) {}\r\n\t catch (ClassNotFoundException e) {}\r\n\t\t return null; }\r\n\t });\r\n\t return super.onCreateOptionsMenu(menu); }\r\n\t\r\n\t\r\n\r\n [1]: http://i.stack.imgur.com/TDamH.png
40	How to specify and make use of header files for verilog language while using exuberant ctags with emacs	I have recently started using exuberant ctags and emacs for verilog & system verilog coding and code browsing. I currently generate the tags using the command\r\n\r\n ctags -e -R --tag-relative=yes --langmap=verilog:.v.vh.sv.svh \r\n\r\nMy code contains a lot of `define macros which are all specified in certain header files with extension ".vh" & ".svh". For e.g. a header file named **foo.vh** has the following code\r\n\r\n `define WIDTH_ADDRESS 32;\r\n\r\nand a file **top.v** invokes the macro as follows\r\n\r\n input [`WIDTH_ADDRESS - 1 : 0] InAddress;\r\n\r\nWhile browsing the **top.v** file using emacs, is there any way by which I can jump directly to to the macro definition in the **foo.vh** file?\r\n\r\nI have been using `M-x tags-search <RET> WIDTH_ADDRESS <RET>` for sometime now but it jumps to quite a few other instances of `WIDTH_ADDRESS in other files before reaching the foo.vh file.\r\n\r\nAfter some research I did see an option to specify header files using `-h` option with ctags during tags generation. However I could not get it to work and I guess there was some syntactical error from my part.\r\n\r\nFirst of all are there any notable benefits of specifying a header file using `-h` option? If so, what is the correct syntax to specify header files? Also can I specify emacs to look into these header files first (files with extension ".vh" &".svh") before parsing other files (with extension ".v" & ".sv")

This output shows GPT model is not exactly working for our use case.

Find similar questions using BERT.

```
#similar questions from BERT
```

```
input=user_transform('do we have any other Q&A platform like stackoverflow
which is free source?','BERT')    #query
```

```
top_n(input,sentence_embeddings,df)
```

	Title	BodyMarkdown
93	Is there an open source Q&A platform similar to stackoverflow?	I need a good open source Q&A platform to boost collective intelligence of my community. The stackoverflow workflow is perfect for me. Do you know of any similar platform?
26	What views can i use in an appWidget?	Can anyone tell me what views can I use in an appWidget?\r\n\r\n Thank you!\r\n
55	Multiple inheritance in C++	As you know, C++ allows `multiple inheritance`. But, would it be a good programming approach to use multiple inheritance or it should be avoided?\r\n\r\n\r\nThanks.
17	can a strong name assambly be used only by a strongly name assambly?	Can a strongly name assembly be used by a strongly name assembly ? I want to know if I signed an assambly as strongly named will it not possible to be used by a simple assambly ? Please guide how to sign a assambly as strongly named ?\r\n\r\n\r\nthanks

If you look at the results, the first question is similar to the one user input query.

CHAPTER 7

Conclusion and Next-Gen NLP

This chapter summarizes various past, present, and future NLP methods and techniques. The chapter ends with information on good research papers on NLP and deep learning.

So far, you have learned the following.

- How to collect, read, clean, and handle textual data

- How to convert text into features

- How to use NLP techniques coupled with machine learning and deep learning to build applications

Now let's look at the recent advancements and the future of NLP. We discuss the following recipes.

- Recipe 1. Recent advancements in text to features or distributed representations

- Recipe 2. Advanced deep learning for NLP

- Recipe 3: Reinforcement learning applications in NLP

- Recipe 4. Transfer learning and pre-trained models

- Recipe 5. Meta-learning in NLP

- Recipe 6. Capsule networks for NLP

But before getting to the recipes, let's do a quick recap.

So far, you have solved some of the most interesting projects under the umbrella of artificial intelligence and NLP.

© Akshay Kulkarni and Adarsha Shivananda 2021
A. Kulkarni and A. Shivananda, *Natural Language Processing Recipes*,
https://doi.org/10.1007/978-1-4842-7351-7_7

You also saw how NLP, when coupled with machine learning and deep learning, helps solve complex business problems across industries and domains.

About 50 years ago, humans began using computational methods for the first time to analyze human language, although most of these techniques have recently achieved success.

NLP is the voice behind Siri and Alexa. Similarly, customer service chatbots leverage the power of NLP to generate personalized responses in the ecommerce, healthcare, and utility sectors. Some of the most popular NLP applications are virtual assistants, sentiment analysis, customer service, and translation.

As technology evolves and evolves, the future of NLP become more user-centric. For example, a virtual assistant can answer more complex questions and assess the meaning and literal meaning of the problem. (Q: What's the weather like today? A: It's rainy. You need an umbrella.) In the future, companies will be able to provide a variety of professional customer services, answer calls and pass questions to real people.

The application of NLP is not limited to solving customer problems or providing personalized advice; it is largely technical assistance. Currently, if you use NLP to ask, "What's wrong with my network?", you can train it to provide a list of errors. In the future, NLP will be able to understand the user's true intentions. The future of NLP is exciting because the advancement of NLP will shift humanity from problem to outcome. It will be a huge leap when NLP understands user comments and provides more sophisticated solutions for their true intent.

NLP will be able to understand human emotions. With the development of NLP technology, computers will extend their current processing capabilities to an understanding of human language in its entirety. So far, NLP has been limited to the interpretation of limited human emotions, including joy or anger. Ultimately, NLP will be programmed to understand more complex human language elements such as humor, irony, and so on.

At an exciting time, NLP will combine other technologies such as face and gesture recognition to create revenue for the business, making it more flexible and efficient.

With Alexa, Siri, and Google Duplex, the next generation of NLP is just beginning.

NLP is also useful for teaching machines to perform complex natural language tasks such as machine translation and dialog generation.

Now let's uncover how some of the state-of-the-art next-generation algorithms would potentially play important roles in the future NLP era through recipes.

Recipe 7-1. Recent advancements in text to features or distributed representations

This recipe discusses recent advancements in text-to-feature or distributed representations.

Problem

What are the recent advancements in text-to-feature or distributed representations beyond what you have learned (i.e., word embeddings, GloVe, fastText, etc.)?

Solution

Distributed representation has been widely used in the past to study various NLP tasks, but the popularity of CBOW and skip-gram models has increased. Most of the recent embedding techniques were discussed in Chapter 3. But keep watch because this space is evolving rapidly.

Recipe 7-2. Advanced deep learning for NLP

This recipe looks at some of the advanced deep learning techniques for NLP.

Problem

You want to understand recent advancements in deep learning techniques for NLP.

Solution

Let's discuss recursive neural networks and deep generative models.

Recursive Neural Networks

The basic form of recursive neural networks, the network function combines components upward to calculate the representation of higher-level sentences. Recursive neural networks are used in a variety of applications, such as the following.

- Parsing

- Emotional analysis using phrase-level representation

- Classification of semantic relationships (e.g., topic messages)

Deep Generative Models

Deep generative models such as variational autoencoders (VAE) and generative adversarial networks (GAN) are applied to NLP to discover rich natural language structures. It is well known that standard sentence autoencoders cannot generate realistic sentences due to unrestricted potential space. The VAE performs a priori distribution of hidden spaces, allowing the model to generate appropriate samples. The VAE consists of a network of encoders and generators coded into the potential space and then generates samples from that space. The training aims to maximize the lower variation limits on the log probability of the data observed in the generated model.

Recipe 7-3. Reinforcement learning applications in NLP

This recipe discusses reinforcement learning applications in NLP.

Problem

You want to understand the role of reinforcement learning in the NLP space.

Solution

Reinforcement learning uses behavioral psychology, in which software agents perform operations in the environment to increase the cumulative rewards of agents. The system attempts to understand behavior over time through trial and error in a simulator environment.

Let's discuss reinforcement learning methods.

Exploration vs. Exploitation Trade-off

Here, the agent must classify the text. The agent determines the next action state through different neural network layers. The trade-off between exploration and utilization involves the dilemma that agents must explore possible behavioral states, which would be useful for legally classifying text and taking advantage of the current state of action to get the best results. In NLP, we should solve this problem by using the softmax function to calculate the confidence limit. Even with unknown uncertainty, softmax and higher confidence limits help to get the highest reward.

Temporal Difference

The time difference concept involves a model-free reinforcement learning method. It is based on the concept that the next action state at time $t + 1$ may be better than the result at time t. This is like the Monte Carlo method. You adjust the weights based on the results. But here, using the concept called a startup, you adjust the results based on the current input before the results are known to get the best results. For example, you want to rank all unknown data. At time $t + 1$, you should be able to predict the label, and in the same way, at $t + 2$, you should be able to determine the next action state. The next step is that you should be able to categorize all the data belonging to the tag and find all other similar tags through behavioral cloning.

Recipe 7-4. Transfer learning and pre-trained models

This recipe discusses how transfer learning and pre-trained models are changing the NLP landscape.

Problem

You want to deep dive into recent advancements in transfer learning and pre-trained models for NLP.

Solution

In simple terms, transfer learning is the process of forming a model on a large-scale data set and then using this pre-trained model to learn another downstream task (e.g., target task). Transfer learning has gained popularity in the field of computer vision through ImageNet data sets. Here, let's not discuss computer vision. Instead, let's focus on how these concepts apply to the field of natural language processing.

Transfer learning is designed to use valuable knowledge in the source domain to help simulate performance in the target domain.

Why Do We Need to Transfer Learning NLP?

In NLP applications, especially when we don't have enough data sets to solve the task (called *T-target tasks*), we want to transfer knowledge from other tasks to avoid overfitting and improve T's performance.

Transfer knowledge to semantically similar/same tasks but with different data sets.

The learning of neurotransmission in NLP depends largely on the semantic similarity of the source dataset and the target dataset.

These are exciting moments for researchers and enthusiasts of NLP and ML. Recently, pre-trained language models have obtained the most up-to-date results in a wide range of NLP tasks, such as sequence tags and sentence classifications. Recent work using pre-trained language models includes ULMFit, ELMo, GLoMo, and OpenAI transformations. These language modeling systems perform extensive pre-training of the entire model using hierarchical representations or graphical representations. This concept changes the use of unary nested words that have been used for many years to process many NLP tasks, favoring more complex and abstract representations.

How does pre-training work in NLP? Why is pre-training useful? It allows models to capture and learn various linguistic phenomena from large-scale corpora, such as long-term dependence and negation. This knowledge is then used (transferred) to initialize and then form another model to perform a particular NLP task, such as a classification of sentiments.

This works in the NLP; for example, negation is an important attribute for detecting sentiment polarity from textual information. In addition, negation may also be useful, for example, to detect emotion or sarcasm, which is one of the most complex and unresolved NLP tasks. Negation is useful in many NLP tasks, so the pre-training model has common attributes.

A language model with generic attributes may be useful in the absence of an annotated data set or language resource in an NLP study. The idea is exciting because we are trying to build a common model and solve some of the difficult challenges of NLP research: the availability of data and language resources.

So far, we know that knowledge gained from pre-formed language models, such as forms that embed words, is suitable for many NLP tasks. The problem here is that this knowledge of potential forms of knowledge is not broad enough or sufficient to properly perform a target task or a downstream task. There are many explanations for this— some things we know and others we don't know—but for now, we briefly introduce one of the latest ways to address these limitations.

ELMo, a recent popular method, is described as "pre-training the entire model using a deep context representation across the stack of neural layers" rather than simply using nested words (one-hot encoding feature representation) as initialization.

The BERT, ELMo, ULMFit. (The way NLP Cracked Transfer Learning)

2018 is the turning point of a text-based machine learning model (more precisely, natural language processing or NLP). Our conceptual understanding of how best to express words and phrases to better understand potential meanings and relationships is rapidly evolving. In addition, the NLP community emphasizes that you can download all pre-trained models like BERT for free and use them in your own templates and pipelines (e.g., ImageNet), showing how similar the development has accelerated the development of machine learning with incredibly powerful components.

One of the latest milestones in this development is the release of BERT, which was described as marking the beginning of a new era of NLP. BERT is a model that breaks a few records and determines how the model handles language-based tasks. Shortly after the model's documentation was released, the team also opened the model code to download pre-trained model versions to large data sets. This is a breakthrough, and anyone who builds a machine learning model that involves language processing can use this powerful tool as a ready-made component—saving time and the energy, knowledge, and resources that can form a language processing model.

BERT is based on some of the most recent developments that have emerged in the NLP community, including semisupervised learning sequences (Andrew Wells Dale), ELMo (Matthew Peters and researchers AI2 and UW CSE), ULMFiT (by the founder Fast. ai, Jeremy Howard and Sebastian Rhodes), the OpenAI transformer (researchers OpenAI Redford, Nara Singham, and Salimans Sutskever) and transformers (Vaswani, etc.).

You need to understand some concepts to understand what BERT is. So, let's look at the different ways to use BERT before looking at the concepts involved in the model itself.

BERT is a stack of transformer encoders, and it has two models.

- BERT-Base: OpenAI transformers

- BERT-Large: A very large model with state-of-the-art results

Both BERT models have many encoder layers (a.k.a. transform blocks): a base version of 12 and a large version of 24. They also have a higher prediction network and more attention heads (12 and 16, respectively) than the default configuration of the transformer implementation on the base paper (768 and 1024 hidden units, respectively) (six-layer encoder, 512 hidden unit and eight attention heads).

A New Era of Embeddings

These new developments have led to new changes in the way words are coded. So far, embedded words have been the main force in how mainstream NLP models treat language. Methods such as word2vec and Glove have been widely used for such tasks. Let's revisit their usage before pointing out the change.

The field quickly realized that it was better to use a lot of text data than form a pre-integration parallel to this often small dataset model. Therefore, word2vec or GloVe can download a list of words generated during pre-training and combinations thereof.

ULMFiT: Transfer Learning in NLP

ULMFiT introduced a way to effectively utilize most of the content that the model learned during pre-training—that is not simply a combination of contextualization. ULMFiT uses language models and processes to effectively adapt the language model to a variety of tasks.

NLP will eventually find a way to make transfer learning possible, like computer vision.

Transformers: Beyond LSTM

The release of Transformers documentation and code and machine translation have led some to believe they are replacing LSTM. In addition, Transformers is better than LSTM at managing long-term dependencies.

flair

The flair framework offers state-of-the-art performance in solving NLP problems such as NER (POS), meaning disambiguation, and text categorization. This NLP framework builds directly on PyTorch.

Most of today's advanced methods are based on a technique called text embedding. It converts the text into a digital representation in a large space. It allows documents, sentences, words, characters to express themselves as vectors in this large space.

flair is an exciting new addition to NLP because Zalando Research's recent article "Contextual String Embeddings for Sequence Labeling" (`http://alanakbik.github.io/papers/coling2018.pdf`) describes a way that is always better than cutting edge solutions. It is implemented and fully supported in flair and can create text classifiers.

Why BERT?

With the massive growth of the Web, we have a lot of data. And only some text data is annotated. We need a lot of annotated data for learning supervised or unannotated data for unsupervised learning for tasks like natural language processing. Various researchers prefer unsupervised learning. They use a large amount of non-annotated text on the web (called pre-training) to highlight some common language representation model training techniques.

BERT is one of these pre-trained models developed by Google that can be adapted to new data and create NLP systems such as answering questions, generating text, sorting text, text synthesis, and sentiment analysis. Since BERT is formed on a large amount of data, it facilitates the language modeling process. The main advantage of using a pre-formed BERT model is that the accuracy is significantly improved compared to the training of these data sets.

The BERT is based on recent work in the context representation prior to training. This is the first deep two-way unsupervised language representation previously formed using a plain text corpus. BERT represents a contextual representation with left and right contexts. It is conceptually simple and experienced. BERT is superior to other methods because it is the first unsupervised deep bidirectional system for NLP pre-training with domain-adaptive features. From BERT documentation, it can be determined that a transformer-based (self-concern) encoder can potentially be used as an alternative to the language model through appropriate language model training methods.

BERT and RNN

RNN (theoretically) gives the infinite context on the left (the word to the left of the target word). But what we might want is to use each of the left and right contexts to see if the word fits the sentence.

RNN is a network architecture for translation and sequential language processing. The sequential nature makes the full functionality of parallel processing units such as TPUs difficult. The RNN encounters a gradient problem that disappears and explodes. RNN has short-term memory because it is not good to keep its entries for a long time.

BERT vs. LSTM

The use of the LSTM model limits the ability to make short-range predictions. The BERT uses Masked-Language Modeling (MLM). The MLM target allows representation of the left and right context, which allows for the formation of a deep bidirectional transformer in advance.

BERT vs. OpenAI GPT

When you apply precision tuning methods to token-level tasks (such as answering questions to SQuAD), it's important to integrate the context into both directions. When using OpenAI GPT, it uses the built-in architecture. From left to right, each token cannot be accessed. The previous token is in the focus layer of transformers.

- GPT uses the phrase separator ([SEP]) and the classifier marker ([CLS]) that are only entered at a specific time.

- BERT learns the integration of [SEP] (special mark), [CLS] (class mark) sentences, and sentences throughout the pre-training process.

- GPT uses a similar 5 to 5 learning rate for all fitting experiments. BERT selects precise, task-specific, and most effective development learning rates on the development set.

The following are some of the challenges.

- Because we have a lot of training data, it is difficult to train even with a GPU; hence, Google TPU can be used.

- The time required for reasoning is long. Therefore, we modified the hyperparameters to make the system accurate and get results as quickly as possible. It has a log for each hyperparameter and chose an optimized combination of hyperparameters.

Recipe 7-5. Meta-learning in NLP

This recipe discusses meta-learning in natural language processing.

Problem

You want an introduction to meta-learning in natural language processing.

Solution

There is an interesting thing in natural language processing (NLP), namely recursive neural networks (RNN), which are used in meta-learning and neural network models.

The behavior of the meta-learner that optimizes the neural network model behaves in the same way as the recursive neural network. As an RNN, a series of parameters and a gradient of the model during training are taken as input sequences. A sequence is an input from the calculation serial output (update set of model parameters).

We have found that meta-learning language models can form articles that memorize recent entries in memory and are a useful starting point for predicting the next part of an article.

Recipe 7-6. Capsule networks for NLP

This recipe looks at capsule networks for NLP.

Problem

You want to get a glimpse of capsule networks for NLP.

Solution

Let's look at what the researchers found when applying capsule networks for NLP tasks. First, you need to understand the following layers and algorithms.

- The **n-gram convolution** layer is a standard convolutional layer that extracts n-gram features at different locations in a sentence through various convolution filters.

- The **primary capsule layer** is the first capsule layer. The capsule replaces the CNN scalar output feature detector with a vector output capsule to preserve parameters such as the local order of words and the semantic representation of words.

- In the **convolutional capsule** layer, each capsule is only connected to a localized area in the lower layer. These capsules in the region are multiplied by a transformation matrix to learn the parent-child relationship. Then a chord routing is performed to create a parent capsule in the layer. The capsule layer is fully connected. The capsule below the layer is flattened in the capsule list and introduced into the fully connected capsule layer. The capsule is passed through a transformation matrix and then passed through a routing protocol to produce a multiplied final capsule and its categories.

- The basic idea of dynamic routing is to design nonlinear mappings. A nonlinear mapping is iteratively constructed by ensuring that the output of each capsule is sent to the appropriate parent node in the next layer. For each potential parent, the capsule network can increase or decrease the connection to dynamic routing, which is more efficient than the original routing strategy, such as the maximum accumulation in CNN, which detects if a feature is present in the text. However, the spatial information about the entity is lost. Researchers explored three strategies to improve the accuracy of the routing process by reducing the inconvenience of some noisy capsules. Words that are not associated with a particular category help the capsule network build a parent-parent relationship model more effectively.

Researchers have already demonstrated the effectiveness of the capsule network in text categorization. More importantly, the capsule network also shows significant improvements in text classification from multi-class to multi-label tags.

Multitasking in NLP

Multitasking can share knowledge between related tasks and implicitly increase training data in the mission. Researchers have explored the performance of capsule networks for text and provided a unified, simple, and efficient multitasking capsule-based learning architecture.

Multitasking (MTL) has been a huge success in the field of natural language processing. Multitasking and deep neural networks (DNN) produce another synergistic effect on DNN through normalization.

Capsule networks can be used in MTL to distinguish features of tasks.

For a deep dive into multitasking in NLP, refer to "MCapsNet: Capsule Network for Text with Multi-Task Learning" at www.aclweb.org/anthology/D18-1486.

Thank you for reading. We believe you had a great learning journey. That is all we have for now. See you all in the next edition.

Index

Printed in the United States
by Baker & Taylor Publisher Services